NEST EGG

· ·

How to Leverage the Knowledge and
Resources of a Financial Planner to build,
protect and transfer your wealth

· ·

ROBERT H. BROWN
CLU, CHFC, AEP®

ISBN: 0615688578

ISBN 13: 9780615688572

Table of Contents

TABLE OF CONTENTS

Chapter Seven: Miscellany

Appendix

Acknowledgements

To be honest, there is probably not a single unique thought in this book. If I have a good trait at all, it is the ability to take other people's good advice. And I have been very fortunate to have had a lot of good advice come my way.

In general, my entire philosophy on financial planning, and specifically, retirement and income planning has been synthesized over the years from widely divergent resources. From textbooks in my college economics courses with professors like Jean Shackelford, to well-known industry speakers like Nick Murray, to my numerous colleagues, I have been bathed in knowledge and wisdom.

The collective experiences of those who have come before us are vast. The amount of new information and understanding that comes our way each day is accelerating. I have tried to distill here the most important ideas, questions, and challenges that face people each day as they plan their way through life.

In appreciation to those who have taught me along the way, I say thank you with the understanding that I very likely underestimate the true debt I owe these people. I apologize in advance for failing to acknowledge those who have also contributed to my development. I know I will miss someone important.

I start with Harry Glah, originally a broker in my hometown. When I was sixteen, my father suggested that I talk with Harry about his profession given my burgeoning interest in investments. Harry was then a broker at Dean Witter in Lancaster, PA. While old time brokers were busy puffing on cigars in the big corner offices, Harry let me sit at his desk, answer his phone, and play with the highest of the new high technology, the Quotron. His unique personality and enthusiasm for success instilled in me an understanding of what the term "client" really means.

Bill Mihm is the man who hired me into the business – a full ten years later – with the very real understanding that I might not survive a year. But his confidence was well placed and his support was unwavering. Jim Grady, Robb Moldovan (who we lost long before his time), and Tom Stroyne all gave me the "straight skinny" right from the get-go and showed me what it takes to be successful at a financial planning career. Virdyn Caldwell has the wisdom of the ages – and the wit and good humor to match.

Paul Anstis, my mentor and good friend, who worked hard, played hard, and was unflappable in the face of all the challenges that life presents, nurtured me. Frank Ausk, the good "doctor," who has always had a big smile, quick wit, and a saying for every occasion, has been a longtime kindred spirit. And Tom Conway, the "large one," whose self-deprecating humor is without peer, taught me never to be too serious about myself.

If there is a kinder and more giving person in our business than Ronna Farberow, I am hard pressed to find who it is. In the midst of juggling her own busy life and business, she not only found time to teach my introductory courses on insurance and investments, but she also continued to provide wisdom and experience well into my 15th year of practice.

Phil Lubinski, a colleague in Colorado, developed the Income for Life program which is the basis for the retirement income planning work we do. Phil's infectious personality and love of a good polka brings a smile to my face. And there is no bigger smiler than Rod McGarry, a mentor and fellow fly-fisherman from Maine. He taught me the all-important party trick of how to pass a plastic straw through a raw potato – among other important life lessons. I am privileged in that many of my professional colleagues are also my personal friends.

My office continued to run smoothly while I took the time to write this book because of my assistant and now office manager Jennifer Davco. When we started working together twelve years ago, Jennifer was a fresh-faced college graduate. Her practicality, determination, and common sense have served her well, and while she is still youthful and ambitious, she has become a most valued partner in our practice. I am very proud of her "promotion" to becoming a financial advisor in her own right.

ACKNOWLEDGEMENTS

Many of the facts and figures seen on charts and tables have been compiled by our interns: Dan Bobick, graduate of Moravian College, Susan Cooper of Muhlenberg College, Chuck Dibilio from Princeton University and Brian Peterson from University of Tampa. I applaud their curiosity and ability to make sense of the complex tasks I assigned them – even when I was not entirely sure myself what I wanted from them.

My daughter, Sarah, now at Tufts University was most helpful at editing this work as well as keeping our office full of youthful fun this past summer.

My biggest supporter has always been my wife, Kim, who allowed me the freedom to start out on this journey in the first place. When I decided to leave graduate school to pursue a job in "financial services" – financial planning as a profession did not even exist at that time – many people thought I had lost my mind. But Kim was ever faithful in her support of allowing me to do the kind of work I really wanted to do, even if she did not entirely understand what I was doing with my time when I left the apartment each morning. She knew that a corporate lifestyle would have killed off many of my brain cells, so she was an enthusiastic supporter of my trying this new-fangled thing called "financial planning."

Of course, my real start came from my mother and father. Where else? They have been the ultimate pillars of support throughout my life, instilling the values and confidence that any person needs to venture into the world. If I turn out to be half the parent they are.....

Forward

When I graduated from Bucknell University in 1986, there was no career option called "financial planner." The industry was "in uterus" at best, but the elements were in place. Mutual funds had recently come into prominence as a ubiquitous method to invest in the stock market. Retail brokers like Merrill Lynch and Dean Witter (now Morgan Stanley) were beginning to reach out to middle class America and introduce them to future superstar managers like Peter Lynch and Bill Gross and to now famous mutual fund companies like Fidelity and T Rowe Price.

The oncoming wave of Baby Boomers, which is the most productive generation in economic history, was generating wealth at an astounding rate. Compounding these conditions was the inevitable demise of their parents who would pass along an astounding amount of cumulative wealth amassed earlier in the 20th century. The final component was the realization that this generation would live a significantly longer time relative to all generations before them. The idea of "personal finance" was coming of age. When enterprising people in the financial services industry recognized the critical intersection of these elements, they stepped into the void and began the "financial planning" industry without really understanding what had happened.

As an economist by training and an investor by hobby, I had an interest in teaching others about what was going on around them. To be a teacher in a professional capacity would have required a PhD for a university professorship. I did flirt with this idea for a year at Carnegie Mellon's Graduate School of Industrial Engineering; however, it became ever clearer to me that what university professors think is important about economics and what the ordinary citizen needs to know about money are two very, very different things.

I was often struck with the same impression my friends and colleagues had about the study of economics. Virtually every person would say that they hated studying economics in school, despised going to their economics classes, and frankly, had no interest in the subject. Yet, they were constantly being bombarded by real life decisions that centered on important economic issues: what mortgage to take out, whether to finance a car purchase, how to pay back student loans efficiently, whether to start a 401K account, what type of insurances to buy, and so on. They found that a lot of their lives in the late 20th century revolved around finance.

My leap of faith into financial planning came in the early summer of 1991 when I decided that the PhD economist track was going to be fruitless for me. Meanwhile, a venerable insurance company that had been in Pittsburgh since 1884 was in the process of taking its own leap of faith into the new "personal financial planning" industry. My experience and training in investments dovetailed well with their vast knowledge in the insurance industry. They needed someone who could understand and explain the consumer's fast moving trend toward mutual funds, and I needed some practical grounding in how to assist individuals in the day-to-day handling of their money. In retrospect, it was a perfect match, although none of us knew it at the time.

The upshot was that I "fell" into the exact job I had always wanted. While I would never be a university professor teaching masses of students about supply and demand or international trade deficits, I would be on the front line of economics. Every day, I have the opportunity to teach people how real world events affect them. What we learn together is not just chalk on a blackboard or a colorful slide on a Power Point presentation. These are concrete, tangible, and ultimately, very meaningful lessons.

For me, there is no better validation of what I do professionally than to see my clients succeed. Whether it is seeing a child graduate from college and make his/her way in the world, or congratulating a client with a bottle of champagne on their retirement, my rewards are far more than simply monetary. Yes, this is an excellent vocation and it does pay well, but the thrill comes from getting to know those we help: developing lifelong friendships with our clients, watching them succeed, coping with the challenges of life's journey, and reaching important family milestones.

Commentators tell us that 80% of all jobs that people will do twenty years from now do not exist today. They will be invented or foist upon us. My wish is that the next generation of workers is as lucky as I am. May they take their passions and abilities into the marketplace of the 21st century and find a wonderful career – or set of careers.

This book is based on now 21 years of experiences in my professional world. My hope is that you can find a connection between the financial issues that you face and the framework that I present. I have tried to break this down into modules, so that you can access specific topics individually. The modules are sequential in hopes that if you read this cover to cover, you will cover the full scope of personal financial planning.

I have interspersed personal and professional comments along the way, no doubt you will see my bias toward having a financial advisor as your partner in this journey. As a financial planner, I realize that this perspective can be perceived as blatantly self-serving. You may choose to see it that way, and if you are feeling cynical at this point, you may wish to reconsider reading this work. Please know that I truly believe that for most people of means, a seasoned financial advisor who truly cares about you will be more valuable to you than you can possibly know.

A professional advisor not only informs you and educates you, he or she thinks about you, worries about you, keeps your situation in mind at all times, knows your family, and understands your business. Your success is his/her success. I hope you will learn at least one important concept or idea that will make you more successful too.

Chapter One

WORKING WITH A FINANCIAL PLANNER

I. FINANCIAL PLANNER

The term "financial advisor" is well known to most people. To say that a person in the financial services industry is a financial advisor is nearly ubiquitous. Everyone from a bank teller to an insurance agent is now referred to as a financial advisor. And in some capacity, I guess this is accurate. Such a person is assisting you (and I hope advising you, albeit often in a minor fashion) on a matter of financial business.

But, such a person is not really a "financial planner" in a professional sense, nor is this person giving the kind of advice that real planners give. In my definition, a financial planner looks at the whole entity – a person, a family, a business – and helps the head of the entity to identify the major financial goals that the entity wishes to accomplish. Then the planner quantifies the goals in terms of dollar values and calculates projected shortfalls and surpluses.

In consultation with the client, the planner charts out several options for achieving the stated goals, taking into account as many contingencies as possible. At all times, the planner builds in maximum flexibility to take account for changing laws, business climates, and personal circumstances. Finally, he/she chooses a game plan and implements particular financial products and services. The final step is a continuous process of monitoring the situation to make sure the strategy is working toward achieving the set goals.

I will outline the actual client-planner interaction in detail later. For now, the important thing to know is that the process is simple, although not always easy. It is simple in that the steps are straightforward and definable. They follow a logical progression. However, the process is not always "easy" because it may take a lot of mental effort and soul searching to define precisely what is most important. How will you prioritize personal and business goals and make decisions on how to balance the use of the scarce resources at your disposal? Will you live for today or save for tomorrow? Can you do both? These can be tough choices.

Throughout the process, however, you will see that there is a terrible price to pay for doing nothing. Procrastination kills opportunity. Battling procrastination and indifference is a very real part of the process. You may perceive that there is no risk in doing nothing now, but with each month you do nothing, you are inexorably closer to failing to meet the needs of funding your child's education, your own retirement, or whatever your particular goal may be.

The good news is that the very fact that you are engaged in the process of planning with a true professional will force you to take some action. Remember, you are not hiring an advisor to do what is easiest; you are hiring one to do what is best. A planner worth his or her salt will never allow you to get to the brink of action and then stop. Once a decision to act has been made, you (and your planner) *must* act. To do otherwise would seem negligent.

In the end, you only have history and experience to fall back on. And history teaches us one thing: faith in the future, not fear of it. As an example, many people postpone investing in great long term vehicles because of short term worries. Headlines and news crawls freeze people in their tracks. Oddly, such "hot news" rarely has anything to do with the future. The sad thing is that the big picture often does not become clear until it is too late to do anything about it.

That's where the perspective of an experienced planner comes into play. Such a person has been looking through the smoke screens of "breaking news" and stock market gyrations for a long time. The big picture remains clear to a good financial planner. The really great planners are your tour guides through the day-to-day morass, so that you can gain perspective on what is most important.

When you come to the crucial forks in your financial road, more good things will be lost by indecision than by bad decision. With a committed planner working with you, bad decisions will be few and far between. In hindsight, we will always be able to identify a bad decision somewhere along the line. My experience has been, however, that more harm is done by inaction than by action that later is seen as a bad decision.

Errors and poor judgment can be changed, corrected, and overcome; indecision and inaction cannot. The question you must answer is this: what will it take for an advisor to motivate you to take the action you need to take to be successful?

II. WORKING WITH A FINANCIAL PLANNER

Despite the existence of a financial planning profession for 20 years or more, it is still very apparent that most people do not really have a good idea of what a financial planner does, or, more importantly, what the financial planning process is like, and what specifically a person can gain from the process. In this section, I hope to outline what the process is like in broad terms. Then we will delve into the specifics of what a series of personal planning interviews is like.

I trust that after having read this book you will be more comfortable with and have more knowledge about financial planning. I hope you will begin to form a series of your own reactions and questions to what is presented. I find that once a prospective client has a framework in which to consider his/her own financial position, the process is no longer mysterious. And once the mystery is removed, we can get to the heart of the matter: planning and implementing your financial future.

As you begin, there are many questions that you might ponder when considering who to hire to help you on your journey:

1) Obviously, you would like to know if the advisor is knowledgeable about his/her field. Specifically, does he/she have advanced study and certification in financial planning issues?

2) Is the firm a good company? Does it have a sound reputation?

3) Is this person well established – both professionally and in the community at large?

4) Is this person in tune with your wishes and needs? Is he/she conscientious, friendly, and responsive?

Apart from these rather obvious questions, I have found that several other issues seem to be equally important to clients, although they are less often talked about:

1) Is the advisor of the same income level and wealth class as I am? Is he/she personally familiar with wealth?

2) What is the advisor's family status? Does he/she have children or grandchildren and will he/she be able to discuss these important financial matters with *your* children and grandchildren?

3) Will this advisor be someone I am proud to associate with? What will my friends or business associates think if it is known that I deal with this advisor?

4) Can the advisor competently explain his/her financial planning process? Does he/she appear to believe in the financial planning process? Is there true conviction?

5) Does the advisor practice what he/she preaches?

6) Will he/she follow the process? Will we have periodic reviews over many years of a productive client/advisor relationship?

If you learn anything from this section, please let it be this: first and foremost, your financial planning should be about you. As such, you should feel free to ask as many questions as you like. There are many people who do the type of work I do – some not as well, some likely better. You have choices, and you should never settle for someone who does not or cannot answer your questions with satisfactory answers.

Part I – The Opening Interview: What does a financial planner do?

While all planners are different in their specific approach, my experience has been that in general, all good planners have a similar style when it comes to meeting new potential clients. While the narrative in this section is predicated on my particular process, the lesson to learn is that you, the potential client, are in control. Any interview process where you feel intimidated or stressed cannot be good for you. This should be all about you, not the planner or the firm. Yes, you want to hear *about* the firm and the planner, but the focus should be on your needs and desires.

Of all the interviews we do, the opening interview is the most exciting. Folks who come to visit us for the first time are taking a chance; we know that and they know that. It can be an uncertain time. Walking into your first meeting, you may be asking yourself, "Can I trust this person? How much of my truly personal information should I provide? What topics do I really want to talk about? And, perhaps, what topics do I really *not* want to talk about?"

From my end of the desk, I anticipate these meetings with great curiosity. I want to learn about who is coming to see me and why they have taken time out of their busy day to talk with me. I wonder about the questions such people will have. Are they nervous, fearful? Have they had good experiences with professional advice before, or have they had some difficult experiences? What are the outward reasons for coming to talk about financial planning? Are there "deeper" motivations for wanting to plan the future? I find this "dance" of personalities to be very stimulating.

Prospective clients have numerous questions on their minds, so I structure the initial meeting as a way for us to get to know each other. Primarily, this first meeting will revolve around your questions. In the end, I have only one goal for that first meeting. When we have completed our time together, I want to know whether we are compatible. By "compatible," I mean do you feel like you can work with me? Will the work I do for my current clients benefit you?

If we have positive answers to these basic questions, we have a reason to meet again. But just as importantly, if we have a negative answer to *any* of these questions, we have also accomplished something. We know that we are not ready to establish a formal relationship at this time. No harm in that. What I want, and I suspect you want too, is closure. Is this relationship worth pursuing, or isn't it?

Since the initial interview is the basis for all future work we will do together, I find it very important to tell you in detail what we actually do for our clients. I suspect that is most of the reason why folks come to see us in the first place. But before we get into that detail, I like to give some background to the business of financial planning in general and to our planning process in particular.

It may come as a shock that only about 5% of professionals in our business are on their way to financial independence. That is, according to trade magazine studies, roughly one out of 20 financial "advisors" who purport to give financial advice about retirement actually has a written financial plan that they actively follow themselves. That's pretty scary. So, an obvious question arises from this statistic: Can you, Mr. or Mrs. Advisor, show me *your* plan? I would ask this question of any advisor – your current one, a prospective one, even myself.

Once you are satisfied that the advisor eats his/her own cooking, you should inquire about the process by which such planning will occur. We use the following:

1) Initial interview (see above)

2) Fact finding interviews (1 or 2 initially)

3) Design and Tutorial

4) Implementation

5) Review and refresher

I will describe steps two through five in detail below. You may have sensed by now that steps two through five are iterative. We are constantly going through the process of updating your financial position, assessing your goals, fine tuning the existing design, and monitoring the progress you are making. This cycle *is* the financial planning process as I see it.

While it would be impossible to cover all the questions that have ever been raised in a first interview, I will try to address some of the most frequently asked ones. They are instructive both from the perspective of common concerns of potential clients and from the perspective of trying to reach a mutual understanding. It is very important to me that we understand each other; I need to know what you want and what you expect, and I believe you want to know the same from me.

One of the most obvious questions is: *How do you get paid?*

In our practice, as in most, we get paid in one of two ways: either through fees or commissions. The primary differentiator is whether we are giving advice only, or whether we are giving advice *and* implementing the plan. More specifically, in the case where we are strictly offering you advice, we charge a fee. Most planners do this either by way of an annual retainer or by the hour, depending on your situation. In most cases, the financial planning fee is eligible for a tax deduction as a "professional fee" similar to your CPA's or attorney's fee.

In the situation where we are giving advice *and* implementing the plan recommendations, it will be your choice. In virtually all circumstances, the products and services we recommend can be purchased through a fee or on a commission basis. There are several differences between the two, but the most obvious is that in a fee based arrangement, you will see the fee being charged to your account and it is thus eligible for tax deduction as a "professional expense." In the commission arrangement, you will rarely, if ever, see the fee. It will be buried in the internal costs of the instrument.

Another common question is: *What products and services do you actually offer?*

This is one question that almost always gets asked at a first meeting. In short, as an independent provider of advice and financial instruments, we distribute products and services for virtually every large financial institution of which you have heard and plenty of smaller ones of which you have likely never heard. Frankly though, this is of secondary importance.

In truth, I am my product. My experience, my knowledge, my intense faith in the future, and my commitment to making clients successful are all included in my product. There is no doubting that you can get financial products and services almost anywhere. H & R Block will give you a loan on your tax refund, Wells Fargo bank will sell you a mutual fund if they think your checking account is getting too large, Fidelity Investments will help you buy an annuity, and some insurance agencies now offer tax advice and filing services. Financial products and services are ubiquitous.

But what you primarily need is not another mutual fund, annuity, or bank loan. What you really need is advice – sound, practical, and useful advice. In fact, only after crafting a game plan with good, solid advice are you ready to begin implementing the strategy by choosing the products and services that are available in the marketplace.

In this sense, we play the role of a doctor first and a pharmacist second. A good financial planner is uniquely qualified to diagnose your situation. Upon diagnosis, the planner adjusts his role to then filling the prescription(s) to treat your situation. In essence, we provide financial solutions – first the conceptual solution, then the product/service solution.

Because we take this approach very seriously, we often have to slow down our discussions with new clients as they are often more accustomed to the general approach of most financial institutions of simply "getting to the sale." Perspective is very important. It is vital that both advisor and client go through the diagnosis stage first and then move on to the prescription stage.

In other words, how you get to where you're going is very important. What's the best way to get to your car in the driveway? Walk to it, of course. The best way to get from here to Boston is to fly – unless, of course, you happen to be reading this in or near Boston. If you are, consider yourself lucky; it's a great city! The best way to get to your basement is to use the steps. And so on. Thus, we must first understand where you are now and where you are going (or hope to go). Only then can we direct you to the right mode of transportation to get you there.

To keep the analogy going, think of a planner as an airplane pilot. I'll help you take off and land safely. I'll get you to the right destination, hopefully as close to on time as I can. You can count on me to take care of the things I can control.

But remember we can't control everything. I didn't build the plane, so we may have some mechanical issues to deal with. And we cannot predict the weather perfectly; we can only react to it. So, there will be turbulence on our journey. The markets will go up and down. You may have several jobs with several companies during your working years. You may have medical issues to deal with. Interest rates may go berserk for a time. These are all things from which we can attempt to buffer ourselves and we can appropriately react to when the time comes.

Let's look at this objectively: If there are two planes flying to Boston tonight, do you want the one with the pilot or the one without one? Do you want a financial advisor to partner with you on your financial journey toward retirement, or can you go it alone?

A final thought before we jump into the second meeting: planners and their firms are not able to satisfy the needs of every person we meet and sometimes we don't discover that until well into our meetings. It happens, but that's OK. No matter what, you should be able to rely on your advisor for these basic courtesies or customer's rights:

1) You are entitled to know what's going on at all times. This includes a timely return of phone calls, emails and whatever new technology communications forms develop over time.

2) You are entitled to at least an annual review, unless you like one more frequently. At a minimum, you should receive at least quarterly account statements that detail how you are doing.

3) You are entitled to timely, accurate transactions and record keeping.

At the end of the opening interview, we provide prospective clients with a questionnaire (see Personal Financial Goals in the Appendix) that helps them organize all their financial matters. We ask them to bring this to the next meeting: the fact finding interview.

Part II – The Fact Finding Interview(s)

Upon successful and satisfactory completion of the opening interview, you are now in a position to decide whether it makes sense to continue this relationship. If it does, then you are ready for the fact finding interview – or interviews. The more organized and direct clients usually cover the fact finding process in one trip. But there are lots of reasons why this stage could take more than one meeting. Regardless of the time involved, the most important part of this process is to be thorough and accurate. Understanding the true objectives and uncovering the essential details of a client's situation can take time; with the proper background, success is much more achievable.

In its simplest form, the fact finding portion of interviews requires us to examine your current situation and consider your long term goals. In my experience, the people who have thought about and wrestled with these kinds of questions ahead of a meeting with any advisor are the people who tend to be most productive. They have serious answers and convictions in regard to these issues, and they have important and insightful questions. Thus, I would suggest that you take some time and really consider what your answers to these questions are. In doing so, you will make quite evident to any experienced financial advisor what your values, morals, and personality truly are.

A set of common questions is listed below:

Common Fact Finding Questions

What is important to you about money? What are your financial priorities and objectives?

What's the money for? Who will use it? When will it be needed?

What's your style? How do you communicate best? How do you like to receive information?

When you think about your retirement/family business/insert-your-most important-goal here, what kinds of things do you think of when you project your hopes 10, 15, or 20 years into the future? What's your strategy for getting there?

What extraordinary purchases/expenses will be needed to create your ideal future? What are your best opportunities to get there?

What are your biggest fears about financial future? What keeps you up at night?

How would you like your children/grandchildren's lives to be when they are your age?

Who are the major decision makers in your family? Do you have other advisors with whom you can consult? Who are they?

With what aspects of your current investment and insurance programs are you dissatisfied?

What is the one area of your finances you would most like to improve?

Looking back at your financial experience, do you think you would have more money or less money if your advisors had been paid on performance?

What are you doing to save money? Why do you save money?

If you find yourself struggling with these questions, you are likely not alone. They are difficult and personal, and in some cases, they are questions you have never been asked to answer before. That's OK. If you are able to give them your honest consideration, any answer you come to, even if it appears somewhat insufficient to you, will be progress.

However, if you find you cannot connect with these kinds of personal and direct issues then perhaps you are not "advisor receptive." But that's alright too. Remember, part of this process is to see if we as client and advisor are compatible. I am not a professional visitor and neither are you; if we find we are incompatible, then we simply shake hands and part ways with no ill will.

These questions, I promise, are the most grueling part of our meetings. I do mean "grueling" in the nicest sense. Clients will often tell me that they are mentally tired after going through a 20-30 minute discussion on what is really important to them about money. Once they "survive" this portion of the interview, then we are ready to move on to the "easy" part.

Aided by a set of current account statements and perhaps recent tax filings that our prospective clients have brought with them, we take the remainder of the time to analyze exactly what these folks have and where it is all found. Depending on the complexity and availability of information, the fact finding may be completed in this meeting or it may spill over into a second fact finding meeting.

After we have completed the true fact finding – both the material what-do-you-have and the psychological what-do-you-think-and-care-about – we are ready to move on to the design and tutorial meetings. It may seem odd, but up through this point of our meetings, you have done all the work. You have gathered your information, you have contemplated and debated the serious questions about money, and you have driven to my office at least two times. So, it's my turn to do some work.

The meeting(s) to follow are the consultation and recommendation sessions where I will give you (and of course explain) a detailed analysis of your current situation and a summary of your important goals quantified with dollar values, savings goals, and a step-by-step action plan for reaching those goals.

Before we end our fact finding meeting, I always ask one final question: Do you think you will become a client? Or, if I am feeling less direct that day, I may ask something like: "Clearly, your situation requires a plan. Would you like to hire me to write the plan for you?"

This may seem to be a rather direct and perhaps confrontational question, but it is essential to ask. By the time we have completed two or three conversations together, spanning three to four hours, I think we both will know if this is going to work as a long term, mutually beneficial relationship. Maybe we have not spoken our thoughts directly, but we will both know. Am I able to help you in the way you want and need to be helped? Do you have faith in me to be a trusted partner in your financial journey? Can I provide you with the valuable advice and support you will need along the way?

If we are not a good fit, we will know it, and we should agree to part as friends at that point. But if we *are* a good match, we will know that too.

Part III – Consultation And Recommendations

From here, it is relatively easy. I will detail in subsequent chapters the particular analytical tools and reports we use to diagnose and prescribe. Plugging in the numbers and quantifying where you stand is not difficult with today's sophisticated software tools. The nuance and subtlety is in the interpretation of the data and then matching up the statistical realities of your financial life with the psychological side of your money.

In general, the consultation and recommendation meetings will go as follows:

We start with an outline of your situation:

1) Review your current position

2) Point out the strong spots and weak spots

3) Recommend and discuss strategies and products that will improve the situation

Chances are, at least one of five things will have to happen for you to meet your objectives:

1) you will need to save and invest more

2) you will need to alter your portfolio to invest more appropriately

3) you will need to adjust your insurance portfolio

4) will need to adjust your expectations – i.e., maybe you will not be able to

   retire at age 50 after all

5) you will need to modify your transfer strategy – i.e., you will need to alter

   your estate plan or beneficiary arrangements

Once we quantify and discuss what needs to be done and you agree with the steps to be taken, we are ready for the final stage: implementation. We verify that savings goals are funded, accounts are established, investments are fine-tuned, insurances are updated, expectations are properly set, and estate plans are in place. From there, we review periodically in light of changes in your life, changes in your intentions and changes in the investment, insurance, and legal worlds.

III. PERSONAL FINANCIAL PLANNING

Introduction

The principal objective of this section is to assist you in properly framing the important questions about your financial future. It is not meant to be an exhaustive survey; rather, I hope to outline the major components of a personal financial plan from the perspective of the "financial planning" profession. As for the more specific financial issues of day-to-day life, like what checking account to choose or what credit card to use, I will operate under the idea articulated by William James in his 1890 treatise "Principles of Psychology." His basic premise is that "the art of being wise is the art of knowing what to overlook." So, I won't be covering what checking account to open or what credit card to use. These are matters of taste and convenience, not earth shattering decisions.

While there are innumerable financial decisions to make along the pathway of life, I hope to accomplish a simple task in this work. My aim is to highlight the vitally important "big picture" issues, and to help you understand them with such clarity so that the majority of smaller, more frequent, decisions and issues seem like "no brainers." If you understand and are dedicated to successfully reaching the larger goals of educating your children, retiring comfortably, and protecting your heirs and your assets, then all other issues that will arise may be dealt with in the context of the larger goals.

Does this mortgage help me reach my retirement goal? Does it hinder it? If I use this money to buy the used Porsche today, does this impede my ability to retire at age 60? Does buying the beach house today put our college savings goals in jeopardy? If every financial decision of consequence is filtered through the screen of a sound, big-picture financial plan, better choices are made in almost all cases.

The Basics

Personal financial planning concentrates on the three main financial stages of life. Understanding the issues and the steps necessary to navigate through these stages is not difficult, but sometimes, life can be. Real life issues crop up; jobs change, marriages dissolve, illnesses strike, goals and priorities change, and so on.

The effective financial plan is therefore made of a basic structure of prudent financial thinking and strategy, sprinkled liberally with flexibility and portability. What I offer below is the foundation for good strategy along with a list of the important issues that should remain at the forefront of your thinking about money. When properly framed, the financial questions that life creates are often easily answered through continuous reference to a good financial plan.

To begin, one should understand that there are three basic phases of financial life (see the Lifecycle of Wealth Chart). You will find that each phase has a set of unique concepts and strategies that typically center on the normal financial instruments and concepts with which you are familiar: investments, insurance, income taxation, etc.

The Accumulation Phase has to do with answering the question: Do I have enough? Or better said, how do I *get* enough? How should I save, invest, and protect my money so that I can do the things I want to do in the future like buy a house, buy a car, educate my kids, retire, and so on? When we first meet clients, this is often the phase in which they are operating. They are attempting to amass the critical amount of capital to accomplish their goals. They are also buying or maintaining insurance to fulfill the goal if they happen to die prematurely or become disabled.

The Distribution Phase is typically the "retirement years." The principal issue is: Will my money last as long as I do? Because we really do not know how long you will be retired, this phase tends to be unpredictable in length and in magnitude. We do know that on average, this phase is lengthening and that most people should plan for a 30 year retirement. Over such time, the most crucial risk folks face is the specter of a tripling of prices. Investments that maintain purchasing power and insurance that provides lifetime income are central to planning in this phase.

The Transfer Phase centers on the question: How much wealth will I pass on to my heirs or to charities? Because the timing of your death is unpredictable, we have to plan ahead for this phase. Proper legal documents like a will or a Trust are essential, as well as a thorough discussion about your plans with close friends or family members. Due to the confiscatory nature of the federal estate tax and the state imposed inheritance tax, good tax planning and prudent use of life insurance can also be integral parts of the Transfer Phase plan.

The vast majority of your financial life is spent in the Accumulation Phase, the period of time over which you are working, saving, investing, trying to avoid taxation, and building your future. It makes sense that most financial publications are centered on this topic in one way or another, yet I believe most of these well-intended outlets for advice tend to be less than helpful.

The problem is that so much advice is centered on specific items and decisions. What's the best mutual fund? Should you participate in your employer's stock plan in your 401K? These are certainly reasonable topics of discussion, but the problem is that it is impossible for a disinterested third party to properly frame the questions on these topics within the context of your personal situation. No one can do this unless and until they actually know who you are and what you are trying to accomplish. Thus, only by your own diligent effort with the assistance of a dedicated financial planner can you adequately confront these issues.

The most effective approach is to begin with a financial plan that presents the big-picture view of what you want to accomplish and when you want to accomplish it. The correct answers to the generic questions "Which mutual fund is best?" or "What life insurance should I buy?" can only be answered when we know what results you want. Put another way, how exactly does Money magazine know that the ABC mutual fund is the right fund for you when they have no idea what you are investing for? Is it the right investment for your kid's college fund? Your retirement fund? Your daughter's wedding fund? If your son starts college in three years, your daughter is getting married in eight years (how would you know that?), and you plan to retire in 17 years, no investment could possibly be right for all those purposes.

What makes a "good" mutual fund or "good" life insurance? Well, there certainly are particular attributes that we look for with all investments and insurances. In any financial instrument, there are some basic requirements that must be satisfied before we can call it "good" or even "best." However, the proper question is not whether the instrument is good; we all have a pretty good idea of what is "good", or at least, we know what we should avoid at all costs. The proper question is whether it is appropriate.

Assuming that journalists and commentators are smart enough to be able to distinguish between what is a bad financial instrument, a good one, and even a great one, this still does not offer the right perspective. We need to be able to say which of the good or great instruments is appropriate for the situation. Let's face it: a $150,000 30-year mortgage at 5.5% from a sound mortgage lender is an excellent choice for a 25 year-old couple trying to buy their first house. But the same instrument is meaningless to an 87-year old widow who needs an income supplement to stay in her home while she receives home health care. It is likewise meaningless for a property developer who needs ten times that amount to finance a building project.

The only way we can properly evaluate the effectiveness of any financial product or service is within the context of one's own financial needs. Specifically, within a financial plan that delineates your goals, needs, and actual financial position, what financial products are available in the marketplace that would be appropriate to use? We throw away the options that are not suitable or effective, analyze the remaining options that could do the job, and choose the one or two that give you the highest probability of success. That's the power of a financial plan; it provides the framework by which these decisions can be made.

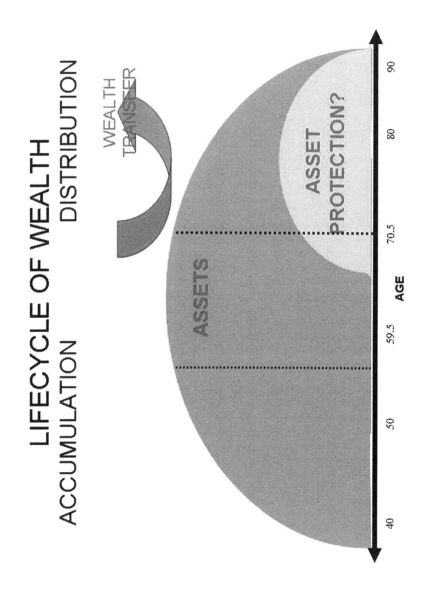

LIFECYCLE OF WEALTH

ACCUMULATION · DISTRIBUTION

WEALTH TRANSFER

ASSETS

ASSET PROTECTION?

AGE

40 · 50 · 59.5 · 70.5 · 80 · 90

IV. FINANCIAL JOURNALISM

Clients often ask if I have seen "so-and-so" on TV recently. "Did you hear what what's-his-name said last night on the 'fill-in-the-blank' business show?"

My answer is almost always "no." I don't watch TV to learn about financial planning; I don't watch Suze Orman (I think the teeth are a little blinding), and Jim Cramer is amusing for 30 seconds or so, but then his ranting and raving gets a little over the top. Frankly, what passes as financial journalism in most cases is really just entertainment.

In all seriousness, do we really need to know where the Dow Jones Industrial Average futures are at 7:30 am every morning as announced by the NPR morning show host? No doubt there are some small number of traders who really *do* need to know, but the average investor who is on his way to work – or more likely on his way to WaWa or Dunkin' Donuts before heading to work – really has no way of knowing what today's Dow Jones futures mean for his retirement fifteen years hence. Indeed, he cannot know, for they are irrelevant.

There are certain aspects of financial management that could be discussed on TV or on the radio. The problem is that they are just not that glamorous. Once fully understood and put to one's own use, these basic ideas are extremely powerful and are the basis for all great wealth. But they do not make great entertainment. "Save 10% from each of your paychecks...." really doesn't play too well coming from the mouth of a half-crazed performer of financial theater.

Increasingly, the "analysis" provided by shows like CNBC confounds me. As an example, I give you the requisite daily report of how the stock market did today, and more intriguingly, the "raison du jour" for why the market went up or down. Countless times I have heard the following blip: "The Dow was up today because of enthusiasm over the increase in consumer spending." Sprinkled in between these throw away phrases, I will hear on a different day: "Oil prices are on the rise and in response, the Dow fell today." On the surface, this seems reasonable and even plausible. More consumer spending means more corporate profits, so stocks should rise. Higher oil costs should shrink profits as corporate costs become higher.

This all makes sense until we juxtapose these statements with the ones made a month or two later — by the same venerable journalistic outlet no less. "The NASDAQ fell sharply today due to concerns over excess consumer spending which was demonstrated by the highest increase in consumer debt load *in four months* (my italics: is four months now a meaningful block of time when it comes to a lifetime of investing)?" Or, try this ditty: "The S&P rose another 1% today on the prospects of larger gas and oil company profits expected to be announced in the wake of steadily rising energy costs."

If the average person tries to make sense of such "knowledge," his or her brain should short circuit somewhere right around the time the next broadcast rolls around, touting this gem that I recently heard: "The market was basically flat today as surges in oil prices and depressed consumer spending cancelled each other out." What?!?!

So here's a basic and simple tenet of understanding the stock market, at least in terms of describing why the market was either up or down in a given day. If the market was "up", it was because there was more demand for buying shares than there was a supply of shares willing to be sold at the current price. It's Economics 101: if demand is higher than supply, the price goes up. *Why* the demand was higher is far more complicated than any news organization could possibly figure out and report on in a fifteen second blurb "on the hour."

The diversion above is not meant to belittle the contributions made by financial commentators. My point is that the average person has a much better chance of succeeding by concentrating on the big picture and avoiding knee-jerk reactions to the meaningless noise of everyday commentary on the "financial news of the day."

Chapter Two

PRACTICAL ELEMENTS OF INSURANCE AND INVESTMENTS

I. INSURANCE

Probably, the only financial activity more boring than reading a mutual fund prospectus is hearing about and learning about insurance. It's just not enjoyable contemplating all the potentially bad things that can happen to a person, a family, or a business. It's just not.

From the outset, I will admit complete defeat, realizing there is very little way to get you or anyone else truly interested in insurance. Though I promise this section has no intention of trying to convert you to someone who *likes* insurance, I hope to help you gain an understanding of the basic tenets of insurance and the solid financial reasons why prudent folks choose to spend money on reasonable types of insurance. They may not like it, but they do it, and when the bad times arrive, they are glad they did. And if the bad times never arrive, they do not begrudge the fact that they were protected all along.

In my planning practice, I have made a conscious effort not to discuss the involuntary types of insurance – homeowners and auto. (Not that you should avoid them, because you should not.) You must have homeowners insurance because no lender in their right mind would give you a mortgage without a protection of their investment in you. And the state in which you reside likely requires you to buy auto coverage if you want a driver's license from them. But like many financial products and services, this is an area that requires special knowledge and experience.

There are many companies that offer these types of coverage (generically called "property and casualty") and they have well qualified folks who can walk you through all the different policies. As you frequently have to renew these policies, you can make changes as necessary. So, find a company that provides good service and someone with whom you can talk to on a regular basis, and you will be well served.

As for medical coverage, this is a highly specialized area unto itself. It is a complicated web of employer plans that change frequently and a government-run Medicare system for those over 65, intersected by your ever changing medical conditions and history. Whenever I encounter a serious situation where a review needs to be undertaken, we refer this out to true experts in the field.

Having begged off the above issue of personal coverage, that leaves only life, disability, and long term care insurance. In no particular order, allow me to present the three major types of insurance you will need to consider throughout your life.

A. Life Insurance

My favorite saying when it comes to life insurance is: Wives don't believe in life insurance; widows sure do.

At some point in almost every interview I conduct with a husband and wife, one of them will make a statement that sounds something like: "I don't believe in life insurance." What the respondent really means is that they do not enjoy *paying* for life insurance. It is as if they are embarrassed to admit they do not want to pay for something they know they really need. Instead of telling the truth, they make a statement about faith, or in this case, a lack thereof: "I don't believe in life insurance."

Well, let's just state the obvious here: you *will* die. Given then that the odds are one to one that you will have the opportunity to collect on your life insurance policy, why would you *not* have one? In the case of auto insurance and homeowners insurance, the odds of actually collecting on either of those is significantly less than "one in one", yet virtually everyone owns these types of insurance.

First and foremost, know this about insurance: insurance is the difference between a real plan and a bet. Without it, you are betting nothing bad is going to happen – and I'll bet your life experience tells you that is not so. If something bad *does* happen, insurance is the only instrument that guarantees a predictable and manageable financial outcome.

The simplest way to begin thinking about life insurance is to attempt to answer this question: If you died yesterday, what would you need your insurance to do for your family today? More specifically, who is going to need money right away? For what purpose will they need it? Who will pay next month's mortgage? How will your spouse educate your children? Will your business survive without your economic contributions? Should your partner buy out your spouse? The questions are endless, and your answers to them are very important.

Whenever you are evaluating life insurance, the most important aspect to define is how much insurance you need. Crude as this may sound, if your friends are huddled over your casket at your viewing, I guarantee not one of them is saying: "I wonder what *kind* of life insurance he had....I wonder what company it was with." Trust me, they are *not* asking that question. They're asking *this* question: How *much* insurance did he have?

I have just tried to bluntly hit you over the head with a large two by four. In case I missed, let me reiterate. How much insurance coverage you have is far more important than what kind you have. Once that is determined, the other details are easily worked out. What kind? How long should the coverage last? What company, etc.? These are the essential elements of any productive discussion about insurance with your financial advisor.

After some discussion, most people will concur that we should determine how much insurance they should have. I get very little push-back on this point. But when we actually do the calculations, most people are floored to find out how much insurance they really should have. They fail to recognize the true economic value of their own worth.

For example, assume you are 40 years old and you make $80,000 a year. Assume you get run over by a bus tomorrow. If you would have worked to age 65, you would have brought home $2,000,000 in earnings during your remaining 25 years of work. That's even with assuming you never got a raise! In truth, your remaining lifetime earnings would likely have reached over $4M. How many 40 year olds do you know who have insured themselves for $4M? Not very many.

People underestimate their true economic value when it comes to life insurance. I suppose it has to do with not wanting to contemplate what it costs to buy $4M of life insurance (which is actually a lot less than you might think for a healthy 40 year old). But I also think that most people don't feel like contemplating their own demise. "I feel fine. Who needs life insurance?"

The only flaw in that thinking is this: if you are in perfect health now, can you get better or worse? Will your health improve or go downhill from today? When are you most likely to get insurance at the best rate? When you are at your peak of health and fitness, is your health going to continue upward or might it be on the downslide? The irony is that people are less likely to buy insurance when they are in fact at the absolute best place and time in their lives to buy it.

Unfortunately, insurance is a lot like a parachute. Once you realize you will need it, it's too late to get it. If you are already out of the plane and free falling, there's no chance to reach up into the overhead bin and grab a parachute. You either have it on or you don't. My point is this: buy the insurance when you know you need it and buy it when you are best able to purchase it at a favorable price.

I will not go into a lengthy discussion on the different kinds of life insurance. In general, life insurance comes in two basic flavors: term or permanent. Term insurance is like renting. You have the least cost of ownership and no commitment to equity. You pay for it as you need it and it ends at a particular time (the term). Use-it-or-lose-it is the basic format.

Permanent insurance is more expensive initially, but it provides additional benefits that may include tax favored accumulation, investment management, flexible premium payments, tax-free growth of equity that may continue to purchase the protection even after you stop paying, and unlimited death benefit. Regardless of whether it is term or permanent, almost all insurance proceeds are paid income tax-free.

One aspect of life insurance ownership that is frequently misunderstood or overlooked entirely is whether the life insurance is coordinated with one's estate plan. One jaw dropping question I often ask is: Did you purposely name the IRS as primary beneficiary?

The obvious answer is "no." Who would name the IRS as their beneficiary? No one would on purpose, but frequently, we find that folks do not fully understand the ramifications of ownership and beneficiary arrangements when it comes to their life insurance policies. Even people of sound mind and body inadvertently allow large portions of their life insurance benefits to get eaten up by income and estate taxes. With proper planning, however, there is very little possibility that this will happen.

How much will it cost? Several variables go into the cost calculation for life insurance. The overarching issue will be your life expectancy. Clearly, age plays a role as does one's medical history. When you buy term insurance, you are essentially making a bet that you will die in that year. The life insurance company is betting that you will *not* die.

Thus, the cost is predicated on the risk that you will die that year. The older you are and the worse your health, the more expensive the coverage will be. Conversely, the younger and healthier you are, the cheaper the coverage will be. Each year, you and the insurance company will decide if you want to play this high stakes gambling game again. If you want to play, you pay your premium.

Because term insurance costs more as you age, many companies have begun to offer "level" term coverage. Instead of starting at a low rate and having the rate rise over time, the "level" term policy will average out the cost over the 10, 20, or 30 year term of the policy. The "level" rate does not change year by year. As an example, a $1,000,000 20-year level term policy for a healthy, non-smoking male is about $1,000 per year. If you are a similarly situated female, you will pay about 15-20% less because women generally live longer. If you are a smoker, you will pay an extra 20-50% simply because of the health risks associated with tobacco use.

In the case of permanent insurance, like "whole life" or "universal life," the basic cost will still be predicated on age, health, and obviously how much coverage you want. On top of this though will be an "equity" portion, or investment component, of the premium. For example, the $1M policy from the above example would continue to have the basic term cost of $1,000 per year, but the full premium on a whole life or universal life" policy with the same death benefit would require a premium of $4,000 to $20,000 in addition, depending on the insurance company. Obviously, the more equity you wish to build and the sooner you would like the policy to be self-sustaining, the higher the initial premium will be.

But why build equity in a life insurance policy in the first place? If we already know that term insurance is less costly year to year than whole life or universal life, and if we know that life insurance is *not* a good investment, why would you want to build equity in a life insurance product?

The most obvious reason is to defray the long term cost of insurance if the coverage is meant to be permanent rather than temporary. Recall that term insurance is cheaper because it only covers you for a set period of time, whereas permanent coverage, like whole life or universal life, is meant to cover you for your entire life, no matter how long you live.

We already know that the cost to insure you against death is obviously much higher when you are 80 years old than when you are 30 years old. Suppose you wanted to make sure your family received $4M at your demise. Buying term insurance at age 30 would likely be the better use of money – first, because the cost of insurance at that age is relatively low, and second, most 30 year-olds don't have a lot of disposable income to "contribute" to the equity portion of a $4M policy. However, by age 80, the cost to buy $4M of insurance – term or any other kind – would be astronomical.

The concept behind permanent insurance is very similar to a mortgage. In a 30 year mortgage, the early payments are almost all repayments of interest with only a small fraction paying off the indebtedness. However, over time, the amount borrowed decreases, which in turn decreases the amount of interest that must be paid each month. As this occurs, more and more of each monthly payment goes toward the principal borrowed and less goes to interest. This process continues in an orderly fashion until the final payment is almost all principal and only a tiny sliver is interest.

By the end of this process, you have built equity in the ownership of your home.

We can also apply this idea to the understanding of permanent life insurance. Think of the premium payment as the mortgage payment and the amount borrowed as the total amount of life insurance. The premium payment is split into the cost of buying the insurance coverage each month (interest in our mortgage scenario) and into the equity (principal repayment). The idea is that over time, part of each premium payment buys the insurance in case you die during that month, and the other part of the premium goes into building equity or "cash value" in insurance-speak.

The upshot of this mechanism is that over time, you make the same premium payment, but more and more goes toward building equity and less and less goes toward buying insurance. It may sound odd, but it's true. If the policy is for $4M, your first premium is buying $4M insurance. However, your 300th premium payment may be buying only $2.1M of insurance since the equity built by that time would be $1.9M. The ultimate payout of your policy is still $4M —the amount of insurance ($2.1M) plus the return of your equity ($1.9M).

On the surface, this may not seem like a very compelling reason to own permanent insurance. Most people who need $4M of insurance at age 30 rarely need it at age 80. So what's the real value of building equity in a life policy? Part of the appeal is that permanent insurance is a "forced savings" vehicle. It obligates you to set aside funds every month (or every year) for your future, the same way a mortgage payment does. It's not always enjoyable setting aside these funds every month while you are starting out in life, but I have yet to meet anyone who gets to age 60 or 70 and says, "I wish I *hadn't* bought a house or a permanent life policy."

The buildup of wealth over time, due to the "forced" monthly savings started at a young age, can be significant. Equity in life insurance products has the added benefit of favorable tax treatment. Earnings are tax deferred until withdrawal, similar to IRAs. If withdrawn before age 59 ½, the funds are subject to income tax and a 10% penalty. If taken after that time, then they are simply taxed as ordinary income. Unlike IRAs, funds from life insurance policies can be borrowed on, usually at favorable rates and the proceeds are normally tax-free. Sophisticated use of these attributes is quite complicated and beyond the scope of this section. I suggest consulting a Certified Life Underwriter (CLU) for complicated insurance issues.

B. Disability Insurance

Over the years I have found that the most misunderstood type of personal insurance is disability coverage. The odd part of disability insurance is that it is the only type of insurance that actually pays you! Think about all other kinds of insurance and who they pay. It's always someone else. Life insurance pays your beneficiaries, medical insurance pays your doctors and the hospital, and long term care insurance pays the care givers and the facility. Only disability insurance pays the insured directly.

One of the often overlooked effects of America's ever increasing life expectancy is that all the major killers of the last generation are now the major disablers of this generation. Although medicine has not eliminated the vast majority of diseases and afflictions, it has gotten much better at treating them so people can continue to live. The result is that many, many more people now live with the conditions that once killed them. But this longevity comes at an economic price.

Living a long time is wonderful if you have assets and income. Living a long time without assets or income can be a nightmare. What provisions have you made for personal protection? Specifically, what is your plan to protect your family during a period of income loss due to permanent illness or injury?

This may not be the kind of question that gets your attention, especially if you are the sort of person who doesn't like to contemplate bad things happening to good people. If so, think of it this way: if you had a goose that laid golden eggs, would you insure the eggs or the goose? I hope you said the goose. Because in this case, you (or your spouse, or both of you) are the goose. You are a money machine, and disability insurance is the service contract on you.

To put it bluntly, how will your income be replaced if you could not work in the event of injury or illness? Isn't it true that there would be little – or at least a lot *less* – money available for mortgages, car payment, investments, vacations, etc? Your income will be dropping just at a time when your expenses are increasing. Your assets will be draining and it is very unlikely that someone will want to let you borrow money, especially if your future earning capacity is severely constrained.

I know what you are thinking. My family can gut it out. My husband or wife will pick up the slack. But honestly, can your spouse be a full time employee, spouse, parent, and nurse? Is this a chance you really want to take?

To answer this question as rationally as we tried to answer the life insurance question, we return to the fundamental issue: how much coverage do you need? Specifically, how long do you want to drain your resources before an insurance company steps in and begins to pay you? For some people, the answer may be "never." If so, fine. You do not need disability insurance. But I suspect the older you are, the more income you make, and the more quickly you would like to get to retirement, the more likely you are to see the wisdom in a well-crafted disability insurance program.

Integrating disability coverage into your plans reduces the risk that a temporary or permanent loss of income due to illness or injury will derail your financial plan. Is it worth taking 1-2% of your income to pay for the right kind of disability insurance to assure that your family won't have to pay the devastating price if you become disabled? Does that make sense? I hope it does because the cost of having coverage is far less than the cost of not having an income.

How much will it cost? Like life insurance, the cost of disability insurance depends a great deal on age and health. The older you are, the more likely you are to be disabled. Likewise, the healthier you are, the less likely a company will have to pay a claim on you. But there are also several other important factors. For example, your occupation has a significant affect on your rate. A psychiatrist or a CPA is less likely to be injured on the job than a bridge painter or a construction worker.

Disability insurance has many unique benefit features. Some plans pay for five years while others pay through age 65. Some policies will pay you if you lose some, but not all, of your income due to illness or injury, while other plans pay only if you lose all your income. Again, the risk an insurance company will have to pay affects the cost. A "residual" or partial benefit feature is more costly than a policy which has only an all-or-nothing definition of disability. Likewise, a policy that pays you if you are unable to go back to your specific occupation is more expensive than coverage that pays only if you are unable to do *any* kind of productive work.

Because insurance companies do not want to eliminate the incentive for folks to work, they will not insure 100% of your income. The more typical figure is about 70%. As a general rule, the cost to cover 70% of one's gross income to age 65 is somewhere between 1% and 3% of the pay. If you make $100,000 per year and you wish to fully insure that income, the cost will be about $700 to $2,100 annually, as this represents 1% to 3% of the $70,000 maximum most carriers are willing to cover.

C. Long Term Care Insurance (LTCI)

Our current generation of seniors will live noticeably longer than their parents did. And we know that the things that used to kill us now just disable us. While the benefits of longer life are commonly understood, this phenomenon of longevity creates a risk. As we live longer, we increase the odds of using up all our funds for medical and personal care. But, where there is risk, there is insurance. That specific kind of insurance in this case is Long Term Care Insurance (LTCI). Marketed by over 160 companies, LTCI is the fastest growing segment of the personal insurance industry.

LTCI is essentially an agreement between you and an insurance company for a pool of money they will pay out in the event you need long term medical care. In insurance terms, there is a very specific definition of when LTCI is triggered. There are six recognized "activities of daily living (ADL)" that we take for granted:

1) Bathing

2) Continence

3) Dressing

4) Feeding ourselves

5) Using the bathroom

6) Transferring (from a bed to a chair, for example)

An LTCI contract usually begins paying the benefit when the insured has lost any two of the six ADLs mentioned above. No matter where you are when it happens – at home, in assisted living, nursing home, etc. – when you lose two of the six ADLs, the policy is triggered.

By "triggered", I mean that the policy comes into active use. Typically, however, the policy does not start actual payments until you satisfy the "elimination period" (EP). The EP is basically identical to the deductible on your auto insurance. You pay the initial cost of a claim up to the deductible amount on your car. Then, if the claim is above and beyond that amount, the insurance company starts kicking in its share. The same applies with LTCI.

When you satisfy the deductible or "elimination period," you begin to collect actual cash benefits. This can mean two things: either you have to set aside enough money to pay for your care during the elimination period, or you have to hope that the initial cost of your medical care is covered by your health insurance or Medicare. For example, Medicare covers the first 100 days of nursing home care that results from any Medicare covered illness or injury. Therefore, most people choose a policy with an EP of 90 or 100 days. This approach allows the LTCI benefits to begin roughly when the Medicare or insurance coverage ends. But, it never hurts to have a good cushion of savings set aside in case Medicare does not cover your initial expenses.

LTCI normally pays in monthly checks based on the amount of coverage you contracted for – e. g., $4,500 per month for three years *or* $3,000 per month for lifetime. The benefit is a monthly amount, payable over a particular number of years, and may or may not have inflation protected increases built in. Obviously, the cost of the insurance is predicated on the benefits you may receive; the higher the benefit (and thus the higher the risk to the insurance company), the higher the premium cost to buy it.

Now, notice that I said "benefits you may receive." Like any insurance, you may pay the premium while all the while hoping you never need to use the coverage. Although most senior clients know one or more of their peers who required long term care, many of them don't fully appreciate the risk of needing long term care themselves.

Statistics indicate that 39% of individuals age 65 or older will require long term care at some time in their lives. If we only consider individuals age 75 or older, the likelihood of needing long term care jumps to 60%. More specifically for the 65 and older crowd, current statistics suggest that out of every 100 seniors, 61 of them will never need any kind of nursing care. Of the 39 who do, 19 of the original 100 will need less than one year's care. Typically, these folks can self-insure the risk. Of the remaining 20 who need more than one year of care, eight will need more than five years of care. Thus, only 8% of those eligible for LTCI are likely to get their money's worth in terms of collecting benefits over a long period of time.

It is therefore very unlikely that you will need to use LTCI if you are a purchaser. The principal question is: can you afford to be one of the 8% who need chronic long term care if it costs $70,000-$90,000 per year? Can you weather that storm? Can your spouse continue to live well if you are the one in the nursing home? Do you want to plan for that contingency or not?

Before you answer, realize that the single biggest risk to your financial well-being in your 70's, 80's, and 90's will be health care costs. These costs will also be the single biggest risk to your being able to leave an inheritance. To go about answering the question of how to plan for LTCI expenses, think about your financial situation and ponder these larger questions. Once you have a strong sense of what's really important to you, the smaller question of whether to buy insurance should be easier to answer.

Here's where to start: if either you or your spouse ever needed long term medical care, could your current income handle the cost? Funny as it may sound, I have a number of clients who actually would be saving money if one of them went into a nursing home since they spend more money as a healthy couple than they would if one of them were in a nursing home. If you are not one of those lucky couples, then think about this.

If one of you needed to enter a nursing home or receive home health care, which assets would you liquidate first? How long could you afford to continue to liquidate those assets? As a general rule of thumb, folks who have few, if any, assets at retirement – say $100,000 or less – are not really candidates for LTCI. Ostensibly, people who need to liquidate assets in large quantity do so because their guaranteed income of Social Security and pension are small. When coupled with few assets, these folks quickly "spend down" to the Medicaid limit and therefore qualify for state welfare benefits.

In the end, LTCI is really for the people in the middle range of wealth. While the folks who have sufficient assets and income can self-insure, the folks at the bottom of the rung have Medicaid to fall back on. Where will you end up? It's always the people in the middle who have assets to protect and who fear being driven into poverty that really need to consider buying the insurance. Does this apply to you?

How much will it cost? The cost of LTCI premiums ranges anywhere from $200 to $500 per month based on your age, health, and the type of benefit you wish to purchase. Regardless of the monthly cost, you are better served to think of the cost in terms of how much principal you are preserving, rather than how much premium is going out the door each month.

While the cost may appear to be, say, $2,400 per year, that premium might be buying $4,000 per month of benefit. If you owned the policy for ten years, the total out of pocket expenses to you is $24,000. While this may temporarily make you sick to your stomach, realize that if you are one of 39-out-of-100 seniors who need some level of nursing care, you will recoup your $24,000 in just six months of receiving the $4,000 per month benefit. Think about that: ten years of premiums recouped in just six months. Should you be in the category of the 19-out-of-100 who receive benefits longer than one year, you will collect far more than you put in.

Another way to look at it is to consider the $2,400 premium as equivalent to $40,000 of your principal earning 6% per year. The interest can pay the premium each year since LTCI costs generally do not change year to year. In this case, even if all the premiums you paid out *never* come back to you, you have likely at least maintained your principal to pass on as a legacy. The nursing home gets none of it. If, however, you went without the coverage and did end up in a nursing home, the $40,000 would be gone in six to eight months......if you are lucky!

Single Premium Impaired Annuities (SPIA). While I will discuss annuities in detail under the investment section, this particular type of annuity is a very specialized product. Sparing the actuarial and nuanced details, these products allow you to leverage a spouse's or parent's poor health to accelerate the income payout. You can do this without subjecting the principal to loss due to premature death.

Think of life insurance in reverse. The healthier you are when applying for life insurance, the lower your cost since the risk that you will die prematurely is small. In the case of long term care, the opposite is true. The less healthy you are, the shorter your life expectancy. And the shorter your life expectancy, the less risk there is to the insurance company since they will not have to keep paying your long term care claims when you pass away. Thus, the same amount of premium buys more benefit when the insured has an impaired life expectancy. Oddly enough, the sicker you are, the higher your payout will be.

The upshot of this economic concept is that good planning can allow you to pay for your care (or your parents') while protecting some family wealth for inheritance purposes – *even* if the person is already in a nursing home. If we return to the case above, instead of needing $40,000 of principal to generate $2,400 annually, you may only need $30,000 invested in a SPIA to create $2,400 annually. The $10,000 difference becomes protected legacy.

Asset Care™. I promised earlier on that I would not plug particular products, but here I am temporarily going back on my word. *Asset Care*™ is such a unique and potentially useful product that it forces me to make an exception. Created by Golden Rule Insurance Company, it is one of the few patented financial products on the market. I describe it as a magical mixture of three separate interacting entities. The specific details are for another time, but the concept is very appealing. When appropriate, this is an excellent instrument, but it may also be overkill, so consider your needs and goals before deciding whether to use it or not.

First and foremost, this is an insurance product. As you now know, it is therefore not necessarily a good *investment*. I have it listed under the LTCI section because it is primarily insurance. For example, if you need coverage of $4,000 per month, the basic policy is a $200,000 policy that pays $4,000 per month when you trigger the policy provision. Since $4,000 goes into $200,000 a total of 50 times, you can now deduce that the policy covers you for 50 months, or roughly four and a quarter years. So far, so good.

As we know from the statistics of LTCI use, the probability that you will actually use the insurance is less than 50%. Naturally, one common reason for not purchasing insurance in the first place is that you may keep paying, but never see any benefit. *AssetCare*™ takes this challenge head-on by adding the second of the three features: life insurance. If you die having never used the LTCI portion, or having used only part of the total benefit, then your beneficiaries receive either the full $200,000 as a death benefit or the unused portion of the $200,000. No benefit goes to waste just because you did not "cooperate" and spend 50 months in a nursing home.

So, we have covered the situation where you need LTCI and the situation where you die without using the benefit, but what about the situation where you never need the care and you live – and remain healthy? The third of the three features kicks in here. I should mention at this point that *AssetCare*™ is not purchased on a monthly basis the way most LTCI is. Rather, it is purchased with a lump sum of cash, typically at some percentage of the total benefit. As in our example, if the cost is 30% of the total $200,000 benefit, your lump sum cost is $60,000.

Now picture depositing $60,000 into the *AssetCare*™ account. On Day One, you have $200,000 of LTCI coverage, a $200,000 death benefit for your heirs, and a $60,000 investment account. The third part of the triumvirate is a guaranteed investment account that typically pays 1-2% above money market and CD rates. In this case, let's say 3%.

At the end of the first year, three things can happen. One, you have needed the LTCI and they have begun paying out $4,000 per month;

two, you have died and the policy has paid out $200,000 (less any LTCI paid out) to your heirs; or three, you have $61,800 in the investment account. Simple math: $60,000 earning 3% adds $1,800 annually. And here's the kick: since AssetCare™ is primarily an insurance product, it enjoys the tax deferred benefits of insurance products. Thus the $1,800 is non-taxable unless you choose to withdraw it.

This triple threat product covers all the possibilities that a retired person might face: long term care, premature death, or long life. It provides insurance for the bad times and a reasonable investment for the good times. Unlike many other vehicles, it also allows you to purchase this coverage with IRA money without making it all taxable at one time.

Most people do not have an extra $60,000 in cash lying around to put into a product like this, but they often have excess cash in their IRA – or they could easily create that kind of cash in their IRA without incurring income tax since IRA's are tax sheltered. *AssetCare*™ can accept IRA money and use it tax-efficiently over many years. For folks who have a desire to cover many contingencies and have significant assets to protect, this can be quite a powerful and effective instrument.

II. INVESTMENTS

At first thought, this section should be the longest and meatiest of the whole book. After all, financial planning has a lot to do with saving, investing, and making money work over a long time. So, you would expect to see a long section on investments – maybe even an exhaustive section on the topic.

Ain't gonna happen!

I have plenty of advice to give, but there are far more eloquent and learned writers on investments out there. While I will certainly make a few comments here and there on certain products and ideas, I will not – in fact, cannot – try to be as thorough and concise as the professional authors and journalists. What I can – and will – comment on is something just as, maybe even more, important: the psychology of investing. What separates the successful investors from the unsuccessful is temperament.

Information is no longer the single determinant in success because everyone has access to the same information. What makes the difference is how the information is interpreted, sifted out, and decided upon. It is on that collection of more subtle and psychological factors that I wish to comment.

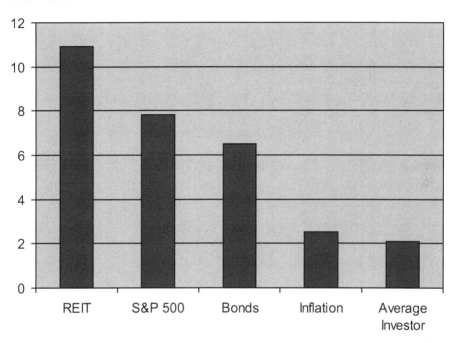

Annual Return by Percentage
1992-2011
Source: J.P. Morgan, Market Insights, 3rd Quarter, 2012

To start, let's look at the findings from a recent study on investment performance versus investor behavior. These results should be remarkable to you! Over a 20 year period from 1992-2011, investor outcomes have underperformed the actual investment performance of the products those same investors use by almost 9% per year in the case of Real Estate Investment Trusts (REIT), and by over 6.5% per year in the case of stocks as measured by the S&P 500.

How can this be? How can an investment that mirrors the S&P 500 return over 8% per year and yet, the average investor, who invested in the same vehicle during that time period, make only slightly over 2% per year? The answer is that the investor's behavior was not logical; it was driven by fear, greed, and any number of other psychological elements. Rather than simply owning the investment and watching it go through its normal ups and downs (but ultimately ups), people bought and sold – apparently buying when the investments were relatively high and selling when they were relatively low.

Before we begin in any detail, let us remind ourselves of the basic types of investments that most ordinary people will own sometime in their lives.

A. Fixed Investments

We start with "fixed" assets. Fixed assets are those items that typically "fix" the principal value and have virtually no principal value fluctuation. These are typically assets you associate with a bank – cash, money markets, checking accounts, CD's, and the like. Frequently, they are FDIC insured so, even if the bank were to fail, all of your principal (up to the FDIC limit of $250,000) would be safe from loss.

The major reason to own such assets is to provide "liquidity" – ready cash for when you need it. Need to pay a bill? Write a check. Need to pay for groceries? Take an ATM withdrawal and pay the bill in cash. We might say that this kind of money is a "parking lot" for funds since it will be spent one day soon.

To be used most effectively, these funds should be earmarked for expenditures within one to three years from today. In addition to being used as liquidity for day-to-day use, such funds also play the important role of Emergency or Opportunity Fund. Most advisors recommend keeping a ready stash of five to seven month's worth of living expenses in a checking, savings, or Money Market account to cover a rainy day occurrence like a job loss or sudden relocation.

But do not limit yourself to just a rainy day fund. Keep the money on the sidelines because you may want it for a great opportunity, like a dream property, a once-in-a-lifetime vacation, a plum investment, etc. In any case, these funds are to be readily available without delay or penalty.

Above all, their primary value is to be available immediately with no risk of principal loss.

Bond Investments. Next along the investment ladder, stepping up one rung, are bonds. There are many kinds of bonds: government bonds like United States Treasury Bills, Treasury Notes, and Savings Bonds; municipal bonds issued by the states, a local municipality, or a school district; corporate bonds from the likes of General Electric or Microsoft; and high yield bonds which are non-investment grade corporate bonds.

In whatever "flavor" they appear, bonds are a form of "loanership" as opposed to stocks, which are a form of "ownership." When we purchase a bond, we are loaning our money to the stipulated entity with the understanding that they will pay us back the amount borrowed, plus an annual amount of interest while we wait for the principal to be returned.

Government bonds are typically assumed to be the most credit worthy of all bonds. The "full faith and credit" of the United States Treasury has historically always been a sign of safety. In fact, the US government has never defaulted on a payment. Whether invested short-term in T-Bills or long term in Savings Bonds, investors are most confident in the ability of the Treasury to pay off the interest and the principal. We expect (and find) that the interest rate paid by US government securities in the form of bonds to be about the lowest in any financial market.

Tax-Free or municipal bonds are a bit trickier. One common question that I encounter with bonds is: Are tax-free bonds better than regular bonds? More directly, the question is stated: "Tax-free bonds *have* to be better than regular bonds, right? I mean, after all, they *are* tax-free. Right?"

Of course, it is not nearly that simple. When it comes to bonds, there are many variables that factor into the equation of what makes a good bond investment. Near the top of the list is always a coupon rate or interest rate. If a bond states that it pays 6%, then the coupon is $60 annually on a $1,000 bond. That's easy – $60 of interest divided by a $1,000 principal investment is 6% interest.

If that was all there is to it, we would be home free. But it's never that simple. Is the bond actually "worth" $1,000 at purchase, or are you paying something more or less? If you were buying the bond for $900, then the interest rate for you as the investor would be $60 divided by $900, or 6.67%. Alternatively, if you buy the bond for $1,050, then the interest is 5.7%. One part of the return, the interest, is derived from the coupon the bond pays and how much you paid to purchase the bond.

However, anyone who has ever owned a bond knows that this is not even half of the story. The "quality" of the bond is another essential part of the equation. Let's face it: a bond issued by the full faith and credit of General Electric Corporation inspires much more faith than an equivalent offering from any company controlled by Donald Trump. This is just my opinion, of course, but it seems much more probable to me that GE would faithfully pay its interest payment and ultimately redeem my principal promise than Donald Trump would.

The "credit quality" of the bond is crucial to consider. Will you get your money when it is due? Will you get *all* the money you are due? Can anyone remember the value of an Enron bond after the company's implosion? I'll give you a hint: it was less than the change in your pocket right now.

Generally speaking, the higher the credit quality, as measured on a scale of "non-investment grade" (marketing-speak for "total junk") at the very bottom to AAA at the very top, the lower the interest rate. The more likely a company or government is to pay back its debt, the less it needs to pay in annual interest to entice potential investors.

If we were to find two identical bonds in the market, differentiated only by the name of the firm that issued them, they should sell for the same price. That is, if all characteristics are the same – credit quality, interest, maturity date, etc. If you have followed this so far, you are now ready for the final leap into the question posed above: are tax-free bonds better than taxable bonds?

The final component in evaluating the investment is the after-tax return. How much do you, the investor, get to keep? If you earn 6% interest but are in the 15% tax bracket, your after-tax return is 5.1%, because after earning $60 from your bond investment, you declared that $60 on your tax form, and dutifully paid $9 in income tax. You "kept" $51, or a total of 5.1% of the original investment. Alternatively, if you could find a tax-free bond, one that paid $60 that was *not* subject to federal income tax, you would earn and *keep* $60, earning the full 6%.

Assuming that you can find two bonds equivalent in all ways, except that one paid tax-free income and the other paid taxable income, the determining factor of which is better is whether one pays more than the other after the tax is computed and paid.

In today's economy and the superefficient markets that trade the economy's stocks and bonds, the difference between taxable and tax-free bonds almost always centers on the marginal tax rate. As of this writing, the critical mark is the 33% tax bracket. This means that two otherwise identical bonds, when separated only by the fact that one is taxable and the other is not, will differ in interest payments by a factor derived from the 33% tax bracket. Specifically, that equation is the yield on the Taxable Bond times the quantity, one minus the tax bracket, equals the Yield on the Tax-Free Bond. So, if the taxable rate were 6%, the equivalent tax-free rate should be 6% times .67 (one minus .33), which equals 4%. At the margin, a 6% taxable bond and a 4% tax-free bond would yield identical results.

This important realization should now make bond investing more straightforward. Anyone in the 15% or 25% tax bracket does not need to consider tax-free bonds since they would make more money for the same risk, even if they have to pay the tax on the taxable bond. This occurs because the gross return before the applicable tax is so high. Alternatively, it makes greater sense for folks in the 35% and higher brackets to consider tax-frees. Only the folks on the fence at the 33% bracket are in the middle ground where the results will be almost identical.

(Author's note: Usually, this straightforward analysis holds for such calculations. However, as I write this in August, 2012 we find the bizarre circumstance where high quality municipal bonds are paying a HIGHER interest rate than are similar quality US government bonds. This is a strange but true reflection of how odd our financial system as evolved since the meltdown of 2008-09.)

The only catch with this fairly straightforward analysis is the Alternative Minimum Tax, which is briefly discussed in the Accumulation Planning chapter under "Tax Advantage." Tax-free bond income can be subject to inclusion in the AMT calculation if you own AMT bonds. Apparent marginal tax rate differences may be compressed or eliminated altogether. This turns out to be a double whammy: lower interest, higher tax. The "flat tax" of 28% imposed by the AMT on "tax-free" income becomes draconian as you are earning the lower rate of tax-free bonds while also being subject to the 28% tax.

Ratcheting up another level of risk brings us to high yield bonds. The term "high yield" is a function of the marketing department taking over the trading desk. What we once called "junk bonds", when such terminology was glamorous, (remember Michael Milken erstwhile occupant of several white collar jails?), we now call "high yield." As they said on Dragnet, the names have been changed to protect the innocent. High yield bonds are within the same unique and valid investment class they were years ago, they just sound nicer now with a more marketing friendly moniker.

As any frequenter of flea markets knows, one may find good junk and bad junk in the market: buyer beware. While a company like Westinghouse/CBS may be considered "good junk," I will leave you to decide where a Donald Trump venture may fall.

Where bonds fit. Now that we have explained bonds in somewhat excruciating detail, we should discuss where they fit into an overall investment plan. Given that most bonds mature in periods as short as 30 days and as long as 30 years, it may seem odd that I find that bonds typically work best in the three to seven year timeframe of an investment plan.

Clearly, you get better returns from high quality bonds than you get in bank accounts. That makes sense because you are taking on more risk by investing in a bond than in an FDIC insured instrument. There is also some volatility in the value of the bond while you own it, and, while it is very likely that the bond will return your entire principal upon maturity, it's not guaranteed. Keep in mind that the higher the quality of the bond, the higher the certainty of principal repayment. This will come, however, at the price of a lower annual interest check, and the reverse is also true.

Though bonds do a good job at protecting principal and pay a higher interest than the truly short term investments like CDs, money markets and the like, they have one major shortcoming. They do not grow. Yes, they provide income and steadiness. And that is important for a portion of your portfolio – in my view, the portion of your portfolio that is 3-7 years into the future. Beyond that, however, the benefits become outweighed by the risks inherent in any bond.

A Short Aside. So far, it would seem we have all we need. Bank instruments and bonds give us safety of principal, competitive interest rates, and a timeframe of up to 30 years (in the case of long term bonds) in which to invest. Why would we need anything else?

This may sound like a basic question. For anyone who has invested in stocks, the question may even sound a bit infantile. But the answer is hard for the folks who have a fear of losing their principal to swallow. There are lots of folks around who have this dread. You may very well be one of them.

The answer lies in the question: What are you afraid of? Or, rather, what *should* you be most afraid of when it comes to investing your money for the future?

We have just covered the situation where the risk is about principal. Essentially, will the investments be worth less than what you started with? This is a very real risk that you must consider with any potential investment. But in my estimation, this is not *the* risk to fret over. For most people, it is only a low level risk; it is certainly not the most important risk.

As discussed in the section on Asset Allocation that will follow, principal risk is very easy to handle. If I may be so bold as to say this: "Please do not worry about principal risk any more. We can come back to it and discuss it again, and believe me, we often do come back to this discussion when the markets get dicey. But for now, please, do not worry about it. There are much more important risks to be concerned with."

Did that assuage your fear? Probably not. I know my simple pronouncement of "please forget about it" will not eliminate or even alleviate your fear of losing your principal. Everyone has this concern, and it is perfectly normal. I merely wish to divert your attention long enough to visualize and comprehend the much bigger and more frightening risk that is looming over your financial future.

Inflation Risk. By orders of magnitude, the risk of losing your principal in a well-diversified portfolio of quality investments is a much smaller risk than the far more likely scenario of running out of money because you have to spend it all. This may sound very counterintuitive. If running out of money is the concern, how can "losing my principal in an investment" *not* be part of that equation?

The potential risk of losing your principal refers to the potential of an individual investment or a portfolio of investments to go down in value. I am most certainly not referring to an investment that goes to zero! No good quality portfolio of investments, including the best companies in the world, would ever go to zero unless some unknown disaster were to shake the earth.

But think about this. If all things went to zero – if McDonald's and Microsoft and Exxon and General Electric and Toyota and [insert your favorite blue chip company here] – if all these companies went to pot, the last thing you or anyone else would be worried about is the value of his/her IRA. We would be scrambling to find our next meal, clean drinking water, and a safe place to simply breathe fresh air.

Clearly, I am not expecting an apocalyptic event. But what I am referring to is the highly probable situation of a newly retired person, living in the United States with normal health, who will live on average another 20 to 25 years. I am factoring in the very real probability that if this person is married, one member of the marriage will likely be around 30 years after retirement.

Such a "normal" outcome, based simply on available life expectancy statistics, tells me that the truly apocalyptic scenario will be the one where our friendly, well-meaning couple will run out of money fifteen years into their retirement. This is the real fear that should be making you uncomfortable when your head hits the pillow at night.

Notice how the possibility of running out of money has *no bearing whatsoever* on the performance of investments. Sure, bad investments may go down in value, or not go up as much when times are good, but even really bad investments will not take you down to zero. What *may* take you down to zero though is the slow, inexorable need to spend more money this year than you did last year because everything you need costs a little bit more. Unless, of course, you happen to be buying health care services, paying property taxes, educating your children, or filling your car up with gas. If that's the case – and I am sure it is – then you will see that the cost of living is rising faster than what our government advertises. The "Consumer Price Index", the national inflation figure, may be a nice sterile number reported on the news, but one need not look further than one's own utility bill to see what *real* inflation is to real people.

The true risk to your well-being in retirement is not of any one investment. Rather, it is the relentless pressure of inflation that forces each of your investments to create and pay you an income. Bankruptcy, if it ever comes your way, will rarely come because of losing principal on your investments (although this does happen to really bad or unfortunate investors). Instead, it is far more likely to come because there was not enough principal available at the outset to support the annual income required to keep you going. Thus, the ever increasing need for more income– more income to simply buy what you bought the previous year, not to buy *more* than last year – is *the* big risk.

The reality is that there are only a few kinds of investments that can address this risk. We now know that fixed assets, like CD's, money markets, and bonds, cannot possibly be the solution. They protect principal only. But, they expose you to exactly *the* risk to fear the most. Radical as this may sound, you must hear it: CD's, money markets, and short term treasuries bonds are the black hole of investments. They will suck the economic life out of you!

B. Variable Investments

If you have stayed with me through that difficult interlude, you must have guessed by now that the only antidote to inflation risk is a portfolio of equities – stocks, mutual funds, separate accounts, real estate, call them what you will. It must be "ownership." You must invest in a stock based portfolio that owns the great companies of America and the world.

Stocks, or more generally "equities," are ownership. They are one of the few engines for growing real wealth – defined as growing your assets above and beyond the constant drag of inflation and taxes. Allow me to be frank about equities: stocks go up. If you were born after 1935, stocks have been going up your entire life. Stocks have always gone up. If you lose money in stocks, you have done something incredibly wrong. Indeed, it takes an immense amount of creativity to lose money in stocks, yet many people do it all the time. The fear of losing money in the stock market paralyzes some people to the point that they never get on, what one commentator calls, the "great train" of equities.

Where I find most people to fail in their stock market experience has nothing to do with the stocks or mutual funds they selected. It had everything to do with the psychology and perspective they brought to the table from the beginning. Let us try to establish some reference points from which to begin our discussion on equities.

Success in investments (stock, mutual fund, real estate, etc.) requires patience and a fundamental belief in the progress of the world. Investing is a marathon, not a sprint. Watching the daily or monthly values of your investments is like measuring a marathon in inches rather than in miles.

It's not a matter of if these investments will go up; it's a matter of where your money will be when they do go up. Will you still be in the market when it booms? Or will you have been on the sidelines waiting for the "right time" to get back in, only to find that the "right time" is after the market has already recovered and peaked?

Where Equities Fit. It is worth noting that true "safety" in financial terms is preserving what your money will buy. It is keeping an unending stream of inflation proofed income coming into your home year after year. This can only be achieved through a portfolio made up predominantly of equities. Certainty is merely preserving the paper dollar you now own. Keeping your principal "safe" in a CD or money market is a delusion – that money is simply "certain". The $50,000 you invest today and recoup three years from now when the CD matures is only "certain" – you *will* get back the $50,000.

But what is also certain is that you are now poorer. In real terms, because of inflation, the $50,000 you get back three years from now cannot buy as much as the $50,000 that you invested today can buy. Simply put, by investing for certainty, folks are deluded into thinking they are avoiding the risk of loss of principal when in fact the contrary is true. The longer they stay in CD's and the more money they commit to these holdings, the more they are accepting (and losing out to) the risk of principal loss. Real financial safety is knowing that within five to ten years, the $50,000 you started with will have grown to $80,000, $90,000 or $100,000. If it can buy as much as or more than the initial $50,000 can buy today, then you are making progress. If it cannot, then you are falling behind.

Put another way: there have always been problems that seem insurmountable, like wars, recessions, presidential elections, etc. There is always a "reason" *not* to invest if you are short sighted. But realize that the people who have continually invested despite the apparent difficulties are now financially secure. These visionaries have come to realize that long term financial security is purchased at the price of the short term – but ultimately negligible – uncertainty of the stock markets.

If you have ever heard a person say he/she could never own stock because it is much too risky, we should be reminded (as should they) that the biggest risk in the great companies of America and the world has always been and continues to be in *not* owning them (see "One Dollar Invested in 1926" chart). Investment losses in the ownership of great companies have always been temporary. Does McDonald's stock value go down from time to time? Surely. And yet, ever more McDonalds continue to be built and each store continues to provide more and more profit to the company's bottom line. A temporary price decline in a stock like McDonalds becomes permanent only when you panic and sell. Over time, advances in the value of the great companies stay and temporary declines vanish. Advance is permanent, decline temporary.

One Dollar Invested in 1926 grew to be how much by 2010?		
If invested in	Your dollar grew to be	Annual return
Small stocks	$14,365	12.2%
Large Cap stocks	$2,590	9.9%
Long term Gov't. Bonds	$85	5.5%
Treasury Bills	$19	3.4%
Inflation	$12	3.0%

Source: Morningstar

Contrast this with the money markets, CDs, and, in this case, the Treasury Bill, which provide an illusory short term security. Once inflation and taxes are taken into account, they simply rob you of wealth and cause, with great irony, long term insecurity.

Short term fluctuations in the value of your portfolio are the inevitable price you pay for superior returns over time. If you do not or cannot stomach the fluctuations, the price you will pay is your long term financial security. For the vast amount of the general public, only equity investments will get them to their long term financial goals and meet their long term financial needs.

I fear I have brought you to a rather uncomfortable point; I apologize if I have. But it is necessary medicine. Rather than making you comfortable with putting your principal at risk, I simply want to make you very afraid of *not* doing it. That does not seem very "cozy," does it? It seems odd that I should be trying to persuade you to re-think your approach by making you more scared about risk than you already are. And, you would be right.

C. Risk Management

Now that I have unashamedly promoted equity investments, let me take a step or two back to discuss some of the more nuanced approaches to how one can mitigate the risks inherent in equity investing.

Face it, there is no perfect investment. To be sure, there are good investments and bad investments. If we could simply know the good from the bad ahead of time, we would surely take the good ones and leave the bad ones behind. Clearly, not all equity investments turn out well for amateurs.....or for the pros. There really *is* risk in this kind of investing, and losses will occur. Nevertheless, there are tried and true approaches which mitigate the risks and which, in fact, can help the risk work in your favor.

A Quick Detour. Before we look at the specifics of risk management, let me take a moment to refine the notion of a "good" investment. I mentioned above that if we knew good from bad, we would always choose good investments over poor ones. But what constitutes a "good" investment?

At its essence, a good investment is one that is financially sound, generates a return commensurate with the amount of risk you are incurring by owning the asset, and stays true to its intended purpose. By this, I mean that the underlying asset should not deviate from its original intention. If you are buying a Utilities based mutual fund because you need stability of principal and a solid dividend, you do not want to open up the fund's annual report and find that what the funds really owns are a bunch of high tech companies that could crash in value.

So, you need investment return commensurate with risk and, you need consistency of style. This is a good start, but we need to do more. We must further refine the set of "good" investments into a smaller subset of what I call "appropriate investments."

Take for example a 35-year old, classic Cadillac in mint condition. Is this a good investment? Well, maybe. If you live in Arizona and are upper-middle class, then maybe it is a perfectly good investment. There would seem to be considerable value to owning it as you could drive around town looking cool. And, you could likely find a willing buyer in the area who would be happy to take it off your hands when the "joys" of car care wear off.

But, what if you are an Inuit Eskimo living on Attu Island off Alaska? I suspect this "classic" car would be nothing but trouble. Certainly it would not be a good investment of time or money. The point is that value is *not* necessarily in the product. Rather, the value is assigned by the person(s) who use and will use the product or service.

Additionally, we must recognize that not all "appropriate" investments do well in all economic circumstances. We need a stable of appropriate investments combining numerous traits and characteristics so that we can create a balanced portfolio. "Balanced" here means a portfolio that has an opportunity to reap the rewards when times are generally good and to protect your principal and income when times are not so good.

Asset Allocation. The technical term for this concept of a well-balanced combination of appropriate investments is Asset Allocation. You probably know this better by a lesson your mother or grandmother taught you many years ago: Don't put all your eggs in one basket.

It is, quite literally, one of the biggest breakthroughs in financial research ever developed.

As we have previously discussed, no investment is perfect. Each serves its purpose in a given timeframe and for a given level of appropriate risk. Extensive research has shown us several interesting facts that are the basis for Asset Allocation theory. And, we can use these findings to our advantage in managing investment risk. Most notably, in every 25-year period of measurable investment history, it is *always* the case that aggressive growth investments have outperformed growth investments. In turn, they have always outperformed growth and income investments, which have outperformed income oriented investments, which have always outperformed cash and its equivalents.

This is almost a law of nature: in every meaningful period of investment experience, the higher the risk (also to be interpreted as "the higher the uncertainty of the return year-to-year"), the higher the annual return is over time.

While we know that you will need to use some of your money this year and next year, it only makes sense that a portion of your investments should be cash and its equivalents, since that is the most reliable type of investment over the short term. Likewise, if you are not retiring for another 20 years, it makes sense to allocate the majority of your 401K money toward growth and aggressive growth investments as they are the only reliable type of investment for that time period. "Reliable" here means that they have the best chance of growing real wealth relative to the inexorable ravages of inflation.

The art of asset allocation is simply to blend the various needs for money you will have over your lifetime with the timeframes over which that money will be invested. The resulting mixture of short-term, intermediate-term and long term investments will constitute your asset allocation.

One fascinating and important result of a properly allocated portfolio is not necessarily all that intuitive. A portfolio allocated across the asset spectrum will almost always produce a higher return over time than an unallocated portfolio, and it will almost always do it with *less* risk. You read that correctly: a properly allocated portfolio will almost always raise the return over time *and* reduce the risk.

That's why in our practice, we do not make any important investment decision without first creating a custom asset allocation for every client. I am so adamant about this that I will not take on a client who does not agree to first create an allocation. In fact, we don't even let clients go to the bathroom without first making an asset allocation plan. Well, we're not that adamant! But it is vitally important.

Dollar Cost Averaging. Once you have the game plan for diversification, how can you begin implementing it to further reduce the risk you face? One of best approaches we use is Dollar Cost Averaging (DCA). Know it or not, you already do this if you contribute to an IRA, 403B, or 401K plan on a regular basis. And that's a good thing because dollar cost averaging works. Here's why.

In broad terms, the stock market goes up in value seven out of every ten years. That's right! History tells us that in any one year, the probability of the market going up is 70%. If we look at each five year period, the success rate goes up to 90%. How can we lose?

Of course, the problem is that the market does not *always* go up. In fact, in most years, there will also be a time when the market drops 10-20% from the highest point during that year. We have already noted that from January 1 through December 31, the market rises about seven times in every ten years. But in every one of those years – seven winners and three losers on average – the market will likely drop at least 10% from its high point during the year. Increasingly, we find that the drop is becoming more closely centered on a 15% drop from the top – at that's EVERY year!

There is much volatility day-to-day and month-to-month. That's why people don't think the market is a safe place to invest. One day it's up, the next day it's down, and sometimes it's down a lot! The fluctuations make potential investors nervous, often paralyzing them from making more investments or worse, to stop investing altogether.

A scary day in October 1987 comes to mind – the market dropped 22% in one day. Panic was everywhere! Yet, had you been in the Peace Corps that year or recovering from back surgery or involved in some other activity that caused you to miss the news of that fateful day, you would have found that the market was actually up that year. From January 1 to December 31, the overall market was a winner, even with that tumultuous, scary, disastrous – but ultimately inconsequential – day.

It always seems that the drops are more dramatic than the rises because losses make headlines and gains do not. The temporary drops in the market make it on the nightly news, but the *real* news is that the trend of the equity market is, and always has been, up. Of course, that October day in 1987 was only inconsequential to those who did not panic. For those who did panic and sold out of their investments, the fact that the year was a net positive was of little consequence to them. They guaranteed their own ruin by failing to abide by the knowledge that all drops in the market, however horrific on the surface, are all temporary. So, if things are so volatile and uncertain, what is a relatively conservative investor to do? The answer may be Dollar Cost Averaging.

When you really think about it, this concept is not all that remarkable. When you go to the grocery store expecting to buy two cans of tuna for $1.99 each, and you arrive to find that the price of tuna is 49 cents per can because of a "manager's special", what do you do? You load up, right?

In every aspect of our economic life, we have learned that when the price is down, we should buy more. Buy-one-get-one-free promotions are very successful because they grab our attention. It's a great deal in many cases; but why then, do we not act the same way when the market is low and stocks are "on sale?"

What is it about human nature that says buy tuna fish, buy an extra pair of shoes, buy four tires instead of the two you really need when the prices are down, but that same human nature says "not only should I not buy more shares when the price is down, I want to sell *all* the shares I currently have at this depressed price?" You and I both know what it is. The simple human reaction to falling stock prices is the fear that things will continue to go down. And down. And down some more until the price is zero.

Of course, as we have already discussed, the great companies of America and the world will not go to zero. They will simply go "on sale" from time to time, just like the tuna fish. But where will you be when that happens? Will you be in the buyers' line or the sellers' line?

The use of DCA forces you – against your human instinct – to do exactly the right thing. By investing the same amount of money every month (or week or year), you force yourself to buy more shares when the shares are cheap and to buy fewer shares when the price is high. It forces you to do exactly what you would do in every other part of your purchasing life.

The people who benefited the most from the bull market of the 1990's were not the people who got in and made their first investments in the 1990's. Instead, it was the people who continued to slowly and inexorably amass shares throughout the 70's and 80's using a dollar cost averaging strategy. Despite the ups and downs of the 70's (mostly downs), the people who had faith that their continued purchase of relatively cheap shares would pay off were more than well rewarded by the boom of the 1990's.

To be sure, in every era of investing, a big dip in stock values is coming. It always is. As I write, both the Dow and the S&P 500 hit their all-time highs 4 years ago and are still about 5-7% below those levels. Have we seen some big dips since the heady days of 2008? You betcha! Will we see more? Absolutely! And yet, here we are closing in on yet another all-time high.

So, the next time you think the market is about to tank, please look at me (metaphorically speaking at this point) and tell me three things:

1) You agree with me: this next dip in the market will happen and it will be

temporary.

2) You know it doesn't matter in the long run.

3) At the very least, you will continue to leave your current assets invested,

continue your DCA efforts, and if at all possible, buy more shares.

If you can solemnly promise me these three things, you are a true convert to the power of Dollar Cost Averaging.

Constant Ratio Transfer. Further research has also shown that a strict policy of re-balancing your asset allocation on a regular basis will further boost return and reduce risk. By implementing a re-balancing strategy, or more precisely, a Constant Ratio Transfer (CRT) strategy, we can systematically sell off the asset classes that have grown larger relative to the others, while using the proceeds to reinvest in the classes that have become relatively smaller.

The asset classes that have relatively risen in value are now more expensive because the prices are higher. Likewise, the classes that have become relatively smaller are now cheaper. By selling the high ones and buying the low ones, we are forcing ourselves to get into the habit of selling high and buying low: exactly what we should do all the time.

Conclusion. Asset Allocation strategies and the implementation of them are useful tools for mitigating the underlying risk of investing in equities. But, sometimes it is not readily apparent. The idea of diversifying is usually best understood in hindsight. An old colleague of mine used to say: "Anyone can swim in waist deep water." What he meant was that when times are good, any kind of investment strategy works – diversified or not. Know anybody who was committed entirely to technology stocks when the bubble burst in the year 2000? I know a large number of employees at Lucent Technologies that were temporary millionaires during the tech bubble because they had committed almost all their holdings to the mother company. And that strategy worked for a while. But, only for a little while. Virtually none of them are millionaires now. See the section on Horror Stories in Chapter 7 for more on this sad story.

Diversity seemed unnecessary when the stock was going from $10 to $20 to as high as $80 a share. But what goes up.....

Of course, diversity shines best when times are worst. The point I am getting at is this: when are you in over your head? When is the water no longer waist deep? More importantly, who will be there when you are in over your head and you are starting to feel the odd sensation of drowning in your own investment pool?

The flotation device that helps you keep above water and paddle safely to shore is the professional advice that comes with an investment plan. A good investment plan has a coherent and reasoned response to important questions. It uses extensive Asset Allocation strategies; it implements Dollar Cost Averaging and Constant Ratio Transfer. So, some obvious questions: do you have a process by which you can select and remove investments from your current investment plan? What is your strategy for diversifying and mitigating investment risk? How will you properly diversify across appropriate asset classes and tax strategies?

Because it is rare to find a potential client who does have a well-articulated investment plan, one of the first things we will do with you is write one. Most advisors write an Investment Policy Statement to define the objectives, clarify the investment plan, and implement prudent risk management strategies. Without this, you are being hopeful rather than deliberate. And, when it comes to your financial well-being, deliberate and thoughtful is definitely better.

D. Annuities

While I promised not to speak too much about individual investments, I want to take some time to discuss annuities. Technically, annuities are first and foremost insurance products and secondarily investment products. If I were being very diligent, I would add this commentary to the insurance section, however, most people are aware of annuities as investments, if they are aware of them at all. In fact, most folks are not aware at all about the insurance component of annuities.

Rather than discuss individual annuity products, I would like to introduce the concept of annuities. It is far more important to understand what annuities do than to understand what they are exactly. If you can grasp the unique properties and characteristics of an annuity in general, you will be on your way to understanding the complexities of retirement planning, in general, and income planning in particular.

Let us say up front that annuities in and of themselves are neither good nor bad. There are bad annuities just as there are good annuities; they are not all bad as the press may have you believe. In fact, the single best retirement plan I know of, the Pennsylvania State Employee Retirement System (PSERS), is built soundly on the foundation of annuities.

Nevertheless, I also hear horror stories about how someone's 85 year old mother was sold some ridiculous annuity that had a 15 year surrender period or a 20 year annuity period during which she earned 1.5% per year. Like any industry, annuity companies span the spectrum from high to low integrity and value. I will not offer any justification for the poor quality companies or the salespeople who sell their products. I merely wish to point out that a well-crafted annuity can play an integral part in your overall investment strategy.

Simply put, annuities are a bet that you will live. Employing an annuity in your financial plan is a positive acknowledgement that you may live a long time in retirement. Annuities pay you to live; the longer you live, the more they pay. While interest rates or investment returns are important, annuities are first and foremost about certainty of income.

The Basics. To understand the workings of an annuity, you must first understand several simple working parts. First, there is the owner. The owner controls the instrument, decides on investments, withdraws money, and makes all transactions. For all intents and purposes, the money "belongs" to the owner.

Next is the annuitant. This subject can be enormously confusing and complex, so for sanity sake, I will stick with the most straightforward and most common situation. The annuitant is almost always the owner. Every annuity has a finite life and the lifetime is measured by the lifetime of the annuitant. In most cases, when the annuitant dies, the annuity dies. This bizarre concept will become clearer when we look at a later example.

The final piece of an annuity is the beneficiary. When the annuity ends, the money in the annuity must transfer somewhere. The beneficiary is the final destination. In this respect, the annuity works a lot like life insurance – someone dies, someone else receives money.

At this point, we have an owner who controls the money, an annuitant whose life "measures" the length of the annuity, and a beneficiary who receives the ultimate value when the annuity ends. But what about the money? What is it actually doing?

Investments in annuities can be one of two kinds. A "fixed" annuity is an investment in which the money is invested entirely in interest bearing funds (very similar to a CD account), which pay a stated rate of interest for a specific period of time. The money is invested by an insurance company on behalf of the owner.

A "variable" annuity is somewhat different in that it is invested in funds that vary. Technically speaking, these funds are called sub-accounts. You will recognize them as mutual funds. A variable annuity is essentially a collection of mutual funds or institutional fund shares organized by a sponsoring insurance company and offered to you, the investor, through their sub-accounts. Instead of owning shares, you own units of the investments. Those units have a net asset value (NAV), and the value of your investment is the number of units times the NAV per unit.

When money is invested in these sub-accounts, the money physically resides at the fund company. If you own the Fidelity VIP Contrafund in your variable annuity, the money is truly at Fidelity. If you also own the Vanguard S&P 500 Index in your variable annuity, that portion of funds is physically at Vanguard. This may seem confusing, as all of your money will be invested in multiple places with multiple companies. Yet, all the money will be reported in one spot. The annuity company is "aggregating" the information from multiple companies and presenting it to you on one statement.

This is an important distinction between fixed and variable annuities. In a fixed annuity, the money is invested by and held at the insurance company. Therefore, you are at risk if the insurance company goes belly up. The creditability of the institution is important since your investment is on the line. In contrast, your investment in a variable annuity provides you with significantly more risk protection against company failure since the sponsoring insurance company holds none of your money.

There are two exceptions, however. Some variable annuities will offer a special account called a "fixed account." Picture a fixed annuity attached to a variable annuity. All the investment options are the mutual-fund-like sub-accounts with one exception. An extra "fixed" account is offered and run by the insurance company. Conceptually, this is a very handy format as you can be entirely invested in the stock and bond market through the sub-accounts, or you can be entirely out of those markets by putting all your funds into the CD-like fixed account. Better yet, you can have any combination in between. Money in the fixed account is subject to the creditors of the insurance company whereas money in the variable sub-accounts is not.

There is one final configuration that I will mention. An "indexed" annuity promises to allow you to participate in market returns when times are good, but pay you a basic (although often very low) interest rate if market returns are bad. In concept, this sounds appealing and many investors are allured by the slick sales pitch. My opinion is to avoid these wherever you go. They are outrageously expensive and often very restrictive. I have never seen a successful outcome in situations involving these products.

Annuities at work. Now that you understand the basics of an annuity, let's turn to the use of these financial instruments. Where is it best to implement an annuity?

Annuities have two significant features that make them worth considering in your financial plan. First, investment returns in an annuity are tax-deferred. Unlike a stock, mutual fund, or CD, investment returns in an annuity are automatically re-invested and incur no income tax liability at the time of re-investment. If you own a CD paying 5% and a fixed annuity also paying 5%, the CD will create taxable income for you while the annuity will create deferred income. You will get a Form 1099 to report the CD income, but you will *not* get one to report the annuity income. During your wealth accumulation years, your annuity investment will offer you the opportunity to build a larger amount of wealth through the tax-deferred mechanism.

Notice I said tax-deferred, not tax-free! You will have to pay Uncle Sam eventually. Annuities are tax-deferred until you make withdrawals. If you wait until after age 59 ½, then you will pay ordinary income tax rates on all withdrawals above your cost basis. For example, if you invested $100,000 in a variable annuity and watched it grow over time to $178,000, the original $100,000 would be tax-free to you at withdrawal, but the $78,000 growth would be taxable at ordinary income tax rates.

One oddity of annuity income tax rules is that the "growth" portion comes out first for tax purposes. In the example above, the first $78,000 of withdrawals would be counted as income taxable and only after you had drawn down the total to $100,000 would that amount then be returned tax-free as a return of your principal or "cost basis." There is one notable and helpful exception to this rule which will be explained in the retirement income section.

The previous discussion of the tax-deferred nature of annuities applies when an individual investor has invested in an annuity that is being funded with after-tax money. The only time that the above tax discussion does not apply is if the annuity is purchased with retirement money – funds from an IRA, 401K, SEP-IRA, profit sharing plan, or other recognized retirement account.

In these situations, the tax situation is dictated by the type of retirement plan. For instance, an annuity inside an IRA account must follow the tax rules of the IRA world. Therefore, presuming that the funds in the IRA have never been taxed, there would be no after-tax money in the annuity. The cost basis would be zero for income tax purposes and thus, *all* withdrawals after age 59 ½ would be taxed as ordinary income. Withdrawals prior to age 59 ½ would be subject to an additional 10% penalty under normal circumstances. There is, however, one significant exemption available to the alert and astute planner which I will highlight in the retirement income section that follows.

The second important feature of an annuity is the inherent quality of being able to establish a guaranteed lifetime income stream. By definition, annuities possess the quality of turning a lump sum of money into a stream of guaranteed income that can never be outlived. The income lasts as long as you do. There is no other existing investment product that can offer this promise.

In essence, this means you can create your own personal pension without the fear of a former employer going belly up years after you retire. Bethlehem Steel employees know this situation all too well. More importantly still, while research has shown us that the longer you live, the higher the probability is that you could run out of money, the same research has shown that the personal use of an annuity as part of your investment mix significantly increases the odds that you will *not* run out of money. It doesn't guarantee success, but it significantly increases your odds.

Why annuities for income planning? The single biggest financial risk any 60 year old faces is living *too* long. That's right! I said, "Living too long." Remember when you were young and wondering how your career would go and how you were going to make enough money to raise your kids and educate them? Remember when your greatest financial fear was not living long enough to make enough money to watch your kids grow up?

Well, guess what? You won that game. Congratulations! But now there's another game, and it's exactly the opposite. What if you live too long? What if you remain on this planet for a lot longer than you thought you would? More to the point, what if you live a lot longer than your money can support you?

Let's face it: the new big financial risk is living too long. Whenever a large financial risk is identified, smart insurance companies move in to tackle it. In this case, the generic form of an "annuity" is the financial product that insures against living too long. If the risk is not living long enough, the insurance is called life insurance. When the risk is living too long, the insurance is called an annuity.

The astute investor might be thinking: How do I put that risk to work for me? Is there a way to capitalize on the good fortune of living a long time without exposing myself to the financial risks associated with long life? The answer, of course, is yes!

Annuities, and their unique form of payouts called "annuitization," have the peculiar characteristic that increasingly rewards you for long life: the longer you live, the higher the payout. The income realized from an annuitized annuity is not solely determined from the amount of money you have invested, but also from your age. More specifically, your payout is based on investment *and* life expectancy – which means the older you become, the more you can leverage your income. As an example, the funds in an account that is annuitized over a single life beginning at age 55 normally pays out a 7% income stream, while the same amount annuitized over a single life at age 85 would pay about a 16.5% income stream on the original principal.

Hypothetical Annual Annuity Payment On $100,000 Invested		
	Annual Payment	Percent of Original Investment
Age 55	$7,026	7.03%
Age 65	$8,379	8.38%
Age 75	$11,066	11.07%
Age 85	$16,614	16.61%

Example based on Life Only Settlement Option for males and representative quotations from high-quality annuity companies, October 2007.

Put another way, annuities are the only financial instrument that allow you to continuously invade the principal without the fear of ever depleting it to zero during your lifetime. And that's not all.

Recall that a variable annuity allows for multiple equity and stock-based choices. Knowing that stock market performance has significantly and consistently outpaced inflation over many years, it is very likely that a variable annuity will not only increase in value, it may also routinely pay out a rising level of income over time. Not only do we have an income we cannot outlive, we also have an ever-*increasing* income we cannot outlive. We may even have principal left over to pass on to our heirs.

Because of this enormously important relationship with income generation, annuities make very good sense in retirement planning, particularly when it comes to defining and supplying a couple's necessary expenses for life. They are not the silver-bullet solution, but they do play an important role in financial affairs during retirement.

Restricted beneficiaries. Annuities offer one other interesting feature that few other financial instruments do. Recall that each annuity has a named beneficiary. Under normal circumstances, the beneficiary receives the funds in the investment accounts when the annuity ends. The beneficiary receives these funds without restriction. However, when there is good reason to restrict the beneficiary's use of the funds, the owner can invoke a "restricted beneficiary" designation that appropriately "ties up" the funds.

Picture the following situation: A widow has an annuity in her portfolio to help supplement her retirement income. She has named her three children as beneficiaries. Her first child is a very successful professional who has plenty of income and a corresponding high income tax rate, but has also done a poor job of planning for the future. He has virtually no retirement money put away for himself. The second child is very responsible, has a nice career, and has done a very good job of planning out her future. The third child is a struggling musician who goes through money like water and has not demonstrated a good track record of financial responsibility, although his musical talent may one day take him far. Should we treat all three children the same? Or, could we use a "restricted beneficiary" designation to more thoroughly address the widow's concerns about each of her children?

Looking closely at the situation tells us that each child has some unique challenges. The "restricted beneficiary" capability of the annuity allows the mother to continue to manage her own affairs under one account, while also controlling the ultimate disbursement of the funds after her death.

If the mother is so inclined, she can fashion the beneficiary designations such that each child will inherit his/her share in the most effective manner. The high income, non-saving son could get his share in a "stretch" annuity payment, which minimizes the taxable income to him while jumpstarting a retirement account for him. The middle daughter, who appears to be the most responsible, can have her money outright so that she can decide her own method of receipt. And the youngest son could be "handcuffed", so that he receives only a small stipend each year (until he gets his financial house in order), while getting "creditor protection" on his inheritance (see Creditor Protection in the Estate Planning section).

E. Conclusion

I realize there is a lot to think about in this section. I have tried to keep the statistics to an absolute minimum. What I hope you have learned is that investing is many parts psychology and process more than anything else. If you keep your focus on the important steps of the process, you can be successful.

I am not asking you, however, to eliminate emotion or fear from the process because it's impossible. What we must not let ourselves do though is act on that emotion or fear alone. We should recognize it for what it is, confront it, and then comfort ourselves in the successful track record of the tried and true ways of risk management outlined above.

Remember these tenets. If you are reacting to every daily market move, you are gambling, not investing. If you are easily swayed by daily market "news", then you are a short term thinker and thus, a speculator. But if you are goal oriented, focused on the long term, and following an investment process based on sound principals, you are an investor. Pure and simple.

By now, you know that this journey is not so easy. Because most of America mistakes journalism for thought, you will be bombarded on a daily, maybe even hourly, basis by silly – and ultimately useless – questions like: Where is the market going? What are the ten best funds to own right now? Are you ready for the next market correction? And so on.

Worst case scenario, you will waste your time worrying and trying to answer these questions. But at best, you will recognize these questions for what they are: irrelevant. I hope you can comfortably ignore these questions, remembering that ultimately, the markets always go up. Knowing which way the next 20% market move will go is irrelevant and impossible to predict. In the end, a 20% move up or down is meaningless for long term investors.

I can say this with certainty: the next 100% move will be up. This is very important, so let me repeat it. The next time the market goes up or down 100%, it can only be *up*. The market will double again and again – likely several times in your lifetime – and it will *not* go down 100%. With this realization, the only reasonable question to ask is: Will you be there when it happens, or will you be sitting on the sidelines?

All successful equity investing is about time – not about timing. Short term swings mean little for the long term investor. Indeed, as a long term owner of equity investments, such short term dips in the price allow you to accumulate more shares at an attractive price.

The most important financial events of your life are certain to come. Your children will go to college and you will need to pay for that. You will retire one day, whether voluntarily or involuntarily. The great financial goals of your life are certain.

No doubt, there is a very real possibility that your stock investments will fluctuate in value over time as you attempt to achieve these goals. Sometimes, they will go down a lot in value in a short period of time. You just have to pick what you are going to be scared of: the very possible but temporary declines in value of a stock portfolio or the certainty that college costs and retirement will come no matter what.

While a sale on the great companies of the world – i.e., a real, but ultimately temporary, stock market decline – is a possibility, you must not be afraid of that. We can hedge against that possibility by using Asset Allocation, Dollar Cost Averaging, and Constant Ratio Transfer. In fact, we can use any temporary downturn to our advantage in an effort to confront the certainty of funding our children's education and our own retirement. The long term upward trend of equity investing, and the wealth it provides, is reward for enduring the very real challenges of a lifetime of saving and investing.

Chapter Three

STAGES OF FINANCIAL PROGRESS AND MATURITY

As we have examined the financial planning process we have seen that it evolves and progresses through a series of stages, each building on the other. Likewise, one's financial journey through life is a series of stages that build sequentially.

After formal education is over and the work-a-day world begins, each person emerges as a unique economic unit striving to make its way. In this chapter, I will outline the 5 basic stages of financial progression (see The Five Steps of Financial Security) that folks typically experience in their financial lives. I will cover the first three stages in detail here:

1) Establishing a firm financial footing in the Accumulation Phase

2) Creating net worth

3) Managing financial success

The final two stages, financial independence and transfer of wealth, are more in depth. This should not be surprising as one's financial situation grows ever more complex as assets increase and financial concerns become more serious. In the following two chapters, I will detail financial independence through a discussion on retirement income planning. Transfer of wealth will be covered in the chapter on Estate Planning.

I. ACCUMULATION PHASE – Building a firm financial footing

My earliest memory of money centers on a childhood friend who regularly saved money from his daily paper route. He would take his weekly collections and put them into 3 piles. The first pile was to pay the newspaper company for his deliveries. Next, he would make a pile for bubble gum and baseball card purchases. This made great sense to me as an avid card collector. Then, he made a third pile which was about as large as the second one. This one I could not understand. He said it was for his Trans Am when he turned 16. I knew Roberto Clemente, Mike Schmidt and Gaylord Perry, but I did not know what a Trans Am was or why anyone would set aside money for such a thing that you could not have until several years into the future.

He eventually turned 16 and bought his used, blue Trans Am. And boy, was he ever cool!

As you can now tell, I have learned a few things about money since those days. And, this first thing I remember learning about money, the deferred gratification that comes from the systematic saving of part of what one earns, is probably the most important lesson that anyone can master.

THE FIVE STEPS OF FINANCIAL MATURITY

ACCUMULATION PHASE: ESTABLISHING A FIRM FINANCIAL FOOTING

- Predictable cash flow and systematic savings program

- Emergency funds on hand, basic insurances in place

- Understanding and using employee tax-advantaged benefits

II.CREATING NET WORTH

- Increasing investment return within limits of risk tolerance

- Reducing the impact of taxes

- Reducing debts and liabilities

- Systematic investment programs

III.MANAGING FINANCIAL SUCCESS

- Recognizing the magnitude of your net worth (estate)

- Effective investment and risk management

- Attainment of important goals: college, retirement

- Basic Will and Trust planning

- Business succession planning

IV.ACHIEVING FINANCIAL INDEPENDENCE

PART I: RETIREMENT PLANNING

- Creating a reliable and sustainable level of income after

 retirement

- Maintaining and expanding assets

- Protecting against loss of purchasing power and taxes

V.ACHIEVING FINANCIAL INDEPENDENCE

PART II: TRANSFER OF WEALTH

- Leveraging gifts during lifetime

- Reducing the taxable estate at death

- Paying the unavoidable taxes

- Sophisticated planning for multi-generational wealth transfers

Establishing a firm financial footing is the first step to financial maturity. In order to do this, you need a reasonably predictable cash flow to start. A job is a good start. But, you can be the recipient of a trust fund distribution or a government payment like SSI benefits or even a legal settlement. What matters is that you have a flow of dollars from which you can begin to systematically save. Like my childhood friend, you need a pile to put the money you will spend to sustain yourself. Then you will need a pile to take care of contingencies like building an emergency fund and to cover basic needs and insurances. Where possible you will want to use your employer's benefit plans as best you can. And, you will want a pile to start building for the future.

In the context of financial planning, this concept is more generally known as accumulation planning. In essence, this area of planning centers on the fundamental question: How do I get enough money? Enough to buy a house, enough to send my kids to college, enough to retire on, enough to buy a vacation home, enough to take a dream vacation, and so on. The simple mechanism is to save part of what you earn, invest it, protect it from taxation where possible and then give it time. At its bare minimum, an accumulation plan is equal parts savings, time, and faith in the future.

Of course, if it were really this simple, everyone would do it very well and thus we would expect everyone to be in perfectly good financial shape. But, given that the

most recent data on retirement reveals that the average family approaching retirement has $99,000 in total assets *including* – yes, I said including – the equity in their home, it is obviously *not* that simple.

The mechanics of successful accumulation planning are somewhat more involved then simply depositing a portion of one's check in a savings account every month.

Both of my children learned to play violin at a young age by using the Suzuki method. Dr. Suzuki believed that any child could learn to play. His description of his teaching method was: it's simple, but not easy. The same can be said here. To achieve success in the accumulation phase, one can follow a simple, well-worn path of tried and true strategies. When taken in tandem, and practiced over a long period of time, these strategies provide an excellent framework for responsible financial management. It's just not always easy to put these into action on a consistent basis.

I call these strategies:

A) The incline of knowledge

B) Financial progression: 3 barrels of money

C) Diversifying tax strategy

D) The bull's-eye of investments

A. Incline of knowledge

Assuming that you are not beginning from abject poverty nor starting from silver spoon luxury, you are starting at some point in between which we may call "comfortable." The goal then is to define a point in the future where you would like to be that is somewhere higher up the incline where all your reasonable financial goals are met. If this were a physics class, we would be defining "work." And, indeed, even in the financial sense, this will be work. Being disciplined enough to save and invest over time will be difficult. We will define your success as how well you can push yourself up the incline toward your financial goals.

FINANCIAL INCLINE OF KNOWLEDGE

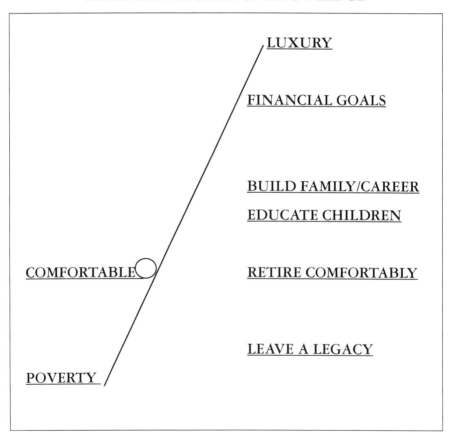

B. Financial progression – The 3 Barrels of Money

I have begun with the assumption that saving some of what you earn for later is a good thing. But, if setting aside money on a regular basis is the task, what is the purpose? What exactly are we saving for? Well, each person's situation will be different and thus, it is not enough to simply save money in a pickle jar month after month. Such savings have to be deployed properly in order to reach the goals.

To understand how deployment can be best accomplished, picture a timeline that begins today at your current age and is spaced out in one year increments. Run the line out to age 70 or more. Now, divide up the timeline into three major sections by drawing two lines perpendicular to the time line. The first demarcation point is generally at a point that is 3 years from now. The second is at age 59 ½. If you have drawn this out on paper, you should have three regions: the first is a 3 year period that goes from your current age to 3 years from now; the second, goes from that point 3 years from now to age 59 ½, and the third goes from age 59 ½ onward. If you are older than 59 ½ then make the second demarcation at age 70 and run the timeline to age 95.

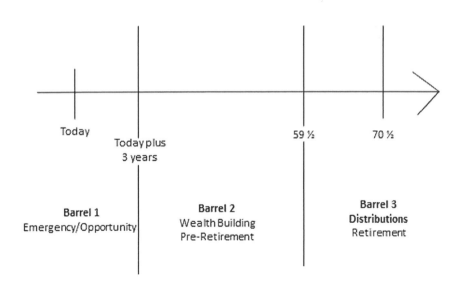

Three phases of financial well being

These 3 time frames define the 3 types, or barrels, of money that characterize a prudent savings (and investment) approach in the accumulation phase. Each of the barrels has unique characteristics and each is important in its own way. If we return to the incline picture, there are two important aspects of financial "work" that must be down. First, we must establish several layers of protection to keep ourselves from sliding back downhill from our current position of being "comfortable." We have defined this as your defense or insurance program. Second, we must then "push" our way onward and upward to achieve a sufficient amount of financial success – however you define that. And this we call the offense or investment program.

I define the first barrel of money as an emergency/opportunity (EO) fund which is fundamentally meant to be a defensive position. It is one of the protective measures we deploy to keep the "here and now" enjoyable. Along with the other protective strategies of using disability and life insurance to keep you and your family in the "comfortable" position you currently enjoy, the EO fund is a collection of cash that keeps you going if times get tough.

Typically, financial advisers will suggest 5 to 7 months of take home pay as a good starting point for this fund. I go a step further and add to this all the money we expect you will spend in the next three years – car purchase, re-modeling projects, big trips, etc. The key to saving for barrel one is to adequately set aside money in sufficient amount to cover the necessary expenditures over the next one to three years and any potential emergency financial situations that may arise.

Alternatively, we can also view this fund as an opportunity fund. What if your best friend calls to tell you that he's going on a round-the-world cruise and he wants you to go but you only have until next Monday to get the money together? Or, what if an excellent business opportunity develops and you want to participate? In any case, whether for emergency or for opportunity, such savings are best deployed when they are in safe, predictable assets like checking accounts, CD's and interest bearing instruments where the principal value is guaranteed – or at least very stable.

Recall that the dividing line between the 2 barrels was drawn at age 59 ½. This is not an arbitrary number, at least not arbitrarily chosen by me.

It could be argued that it was arbitrarily chosen by Congress when it chose the age to define the tax law surrounding IRA's and 401K's. Regardless, money that is available for use prior to age 59 ½ (barrel 2) is generally taxable as it grows while money in barrel 3 is typically tax-favored until its withdrawal; however, barrel 3 money is generally "hands off" until that peculiar age of 59 1/2. Otherwise a 10% premature withdrawal penalty is imposed in addition to normal income tax.

If we characterize the first barrel as "defensive" money, then certainly barrels 2 and 3 are "offense." More specifically, these barrels are for the money that will be invested in growth oriented instruments like stocks and stock-based mutual funds; these investments will "push" you up the incline. They are designed to build real wealth above and beyond the annual ravages of inflation. The principal difference between the two will be whether or not the money is tax-favored for retirement.

Thus, we have the three types of savings: an emergency/opportunity fund which is primarily defensive in nature, an investment pool that is generally available for use and therefore taxable year-by-year, and an investment pool that is tax-favored in return for an agreement that you will not touch it until many years from now. The key then is to properly allocate your monthly savings in order to properly "fill" each of the barrels.

Above, I have defined the method by which you determine the amount required in barrel one: five to seven months of take home pay plus the spending for large ticket items that you know you will buy in the next 1 to 3 years. Calculating what you need for barrels 2 and 3 is determined entirely by what particular goals you have for yourself, your current age, when the goals need to be reached and your family situation. In later sections, I will delineate the largest of the goals for most people: college/education funding typically for barrel 2 and retirement planning for barrel 3.

We might sum up this timeline approach to the barrels of money by looking at the general trajectory of a normal economic life in America. While you are building your career in your 30's, you may also be building and furnishing a house with spending that typically comes from barrel 1. In your 40's, you are building up your children and writing their tuition checks (barrel 2 money). In your 50's you begin to get serious about retirement (rebuilding your barrel 2). In your 60's and 70's you will focus your energy on enjoying your own retirement (and thus using barrel 3 money). Beyond that, you begin to look at your legacy – what you will leave to your children, grandchildren and charity. Because you will spend a lot of money over your lifetime, you need to put *away* a lot of money during your working years and, you will need to put those funds into all 3 barrels.

C. Diversifying tax strategy

The simple fact that Ben Franklin pointed out two centuries ago is still true today: a penny saved is a penny earned. Although, had there been income taxes in his day, it is likely Ben would have added a corollary: a penny in tax saved is a penny earned. Every time your savings and investments are taxed, you take a step back from your final goal. Thus, investing with an eye toward tax efficiency is paramount.

Obviously, there is significant opportunity to protect investment income from taxation in barrel 3 since it is, by its character, a tax-favored environment. Whether you have a Roth IRA, Traditional IRA, 403B plan, Tax Sheltered Annuity, or any other retirement instrument, it is all barrel 3 money and it is all tax-favored. All other things being equal then, we would expect an IRA or a Roth IRA invested in a mutual fund and starting off at $100,000 to be worth more than the exact same fund, also starting off at $100,000, but invested in a personal brokerage account. The one and only reason is that the brokerage account will be taxed year by year and the IRA will not.

It is more difficult to get favorable tax treatment on savings and investments in barrels one and two (see the section on Tax Free Bonds); although, there are well trod paths in this area to get favorable tax treatment including tax-free money markets, variable life insurance and US Savings bonds. Likewise there is some tax deferral on instruments like individual stocks and mutual funds although they are ultimately taxable upon sale.

While one endeavors to diversify one's investments to take advantage of changing currents across different markets, it also makes sense to consider diversifying your tax strategy. Having money deployed across barrels one through three not only properly allocates money to the specific tasks to be accomplished in those timeframes, but it also allows you to spread out the tax liabilities across time. When you need to "harvest" some of your investments in the future, one aspect of the decision on which investment to sell will be what the tax consequences are. Since we do not know with any great accuracy what our friends in Congress will be doing with the tax code over the next 5 and 10 years, it is always good to have several different strategies at work. That way, no matter which way the laws change, you will always have an instrument that is treated more favorably than the others you may own.

A final word on taxes here: do not let the tail wag the dog! Too many times people make bad financial decisions based solely on the tax consequences of the decision. Taxes are important but they are not the *most* important. Reaching your overall goal, following a long term plan and being faithful to your saving targets are all far more important. When folks tell me that they do not want to pay any taxes, I generally respond this way: "My job is to give you the biggest tax bill you ever had. It's a sign of success! I know a lot of guys who can give you tax write-offs – i.e., losses. Want to meet them? I suspect not."

Alternative Minimum Tax. In addition to the standard income tax brackets with which most of us are familiar, there is a second tax structure that more and more people are coming to understand. It's called the Alternative Minimum Tax (AMT) and few, if any, who are subject to it relish the term. In fact, it is one of the most dreaded subjects for a CPA to introduce to a client at tax filing time. "I'm sorry Mr. and Mrs. Client but, despite our best efforts, it looks like you will be subject to the AMT this year."

The AMT was created with the best of intentions; the goal was to target a very small number of high-income households that used so many tax loopholes that they owed little or no income tax. The goal was to impose a blanket, flat tax (around 28%) on these households so that they would pay their fair share of taxes while the rest of us paid under the normal regime.

Suffice to say, as with any government bureaucracy, "things got out of hand." Now, hundreds of thousands of taxpayers are caught up in the AMT which has grown into a convoluted formula of "tax preference items" like long-term capital gains, depreciation, medical expenses, depletion allowances, tax-exempt income, credits, exemptions and the odd kitchen sink.

Because the AMT is not indexed to inflation, the upshot is that an increasing number of middle-income taxpayers are subject to this tax. Only your tax preparer can truly give this topic justice as they struggle with it every day. For purposes of this discussion, I am assuming you are *not* subject to AMT. From the standpoint of our individual planning work, we endeavor to avoid AMT wherever possible.

D. The Bull's-eye of investments

While there is plenty of material on investments throughout this book, I want to focus specifically here on how investments are priced. It is important to understand the "layers" of expenses associated with investments and the general costs that are imposed on the investor. More specifically, I want to focus on whether the cost incurred is worth the benefit offered. To explain this, I generally reference a drawing that looks like an archery bull's eye.

In the center is you, the investor. What we ultimately are focusing on is the amount of return you get. If you look in the newspaper and it says that your mutual fund returned 8% then that's what you, the investor, received. If you put in $1,000 to start then you should now have $1,080. Virtually everything that you see will be quoted in terms of the return you got. The prospectus will show this number, the newspaper will show it,

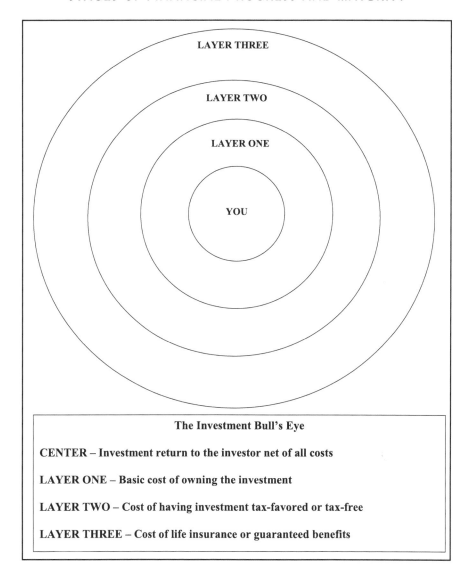

The Investment Bull's Eye

CENTER – Investment return to the investor net of all costs

LAYER ONE – Basic cost of owning the investment

LAYER TWO – Cost of having investment tax-favored or tax-free

LAYER THREE – Cost of life insurance or guaranteed benefits

your statement will show it, and so on. They will all reference this number. And yet, the investment actually made more that. Here's why: there are several layers of expenses built on top of what you actually get to keep.

Layer 1. The first layer of expense around the bull's eye to understand is the basic cost of owning the investment. In the mutual fund example, there are a variety of costs that may be incurred. Principally, the management fee is the largest portion of the cost; it covers the cost to run the fund, pay all the people at the fund company who administer and service the shareholders and who do the investment research. But, there can also be marketing, distribution and redemption fees, 12-B-1 fees and other miscellaneous costs. In the end, the total of all these otherwise unseen costs is "shaved" off the top.

While it would seem that a CD or a checking account (if it is "no fee") has no cost, you would be very wrong to think this. Bank assets are also subject to expense in layer one. In fact, there is actually quite a price for these assets – albeit not an out-of-pocket expense.

One useful way to figure the cost to you is to look at what the bank will do with the money. How much will they make with your cash? Assuming that they take your checking account money, pool it together with everyone else's checking account money and package it up into a loan, what can they charge for the loan? Well, assume that you needed a mortgage, what would the bank charge you? Let's say 7%.

We can then say that the "cost" of owning a bank account or CD is the 7% revenue the bank receives (by turning around and loaning out money; that's what the money earns in the marketplace) less the interest you are earning on your checking account. If you are getting one percent then the "cost" of the investment is 6%. If they are paying you 4% on a CD, then the cost to you is 3%.

Is it any wonder that great investors would always rather *own* the bank than merely "invest" in the bank? Clearly the return is high to the bank and the unwritten, but nevertheless very real, cost to you as the depositor is likewise as high.

Now, if we wish to attempt to make more money than we can get in a bank, we know we need to look at other instruments. Let us now return to the mutual fund example with which we started this discussion. If you see that your investment return was 8% and you know that the total management costs were 1.25%, then you can rightly calculate that the true return was the sum of the two or 9.25%.

As we look at the bull's eye imagery, the concept is that with each additional "layer" of benefit accrued to the investor, we should expect an additional layer of expense. The first layer is generically known as "professional investment oversight" provided by either a money manager in the case of a mutual fund or by a bank in the CD case. If we were to use individual stocks and bonds instead, then the layer of cost would include brokerage, trading and or account fees.

Layer 2. If we expand outward into a second layer of expense, we arrive at tax favored investing. In case you didn't already know, the benefit of tax-favored investment generally comes with an additional layer of expense. For example, as a participant in a 401k plan, the costs are two-fold: the professional management fee payable to the fund managers who run each investment choice (layer 1) and the administrative fees of installing, running, testing and filing the plan with the IRS (layer 2). While it may be true that your company covers the cost in lieu of the employees paying, it is still true that a tax-favored instrument like a 401K plan is a 2-layered instrument.

There are other, more subtle distinctions in this idea of multi-layered costs. Take a municipal bond fund for example. In addition to the layer 1 expenses of the professional money managers running the fund, there is a second "layer" of cost exacted by the market on the dividend yield. For example, a fund investing in United States Treasuries (income from which is fully taxable on the federal level) will always pay more interest than a comparable fund of tax-free municipals because every investor knows that the municipal bond income will be tax-free. Thus, such a bond fund need only pay an amount of tax-free income equivalent to the "after-tax" amount of Treasury income to be competitive (see the previous chapter on tax-free bonds). Even though this cost is not paid to anyone directly, it is indeed a cost of investing in the tax-favored instrument known as municipal bonds. (Author's note: We live in strange times. As I write this, high grade municipal bonds actually pay more interest than the 10 year Treasury bond. This is *not* normal!)

Insurance related instruments tend to span across layers 2 and 3. A fixed annuity that pays a stated rate of interest at a tax-deferred rate, is clearly a layer 2 vehicle as the costs are similar to the CD example: what the insurance company can make on your deposit less what they pay you in interest on the annuity (layer 1) and an additional amount payable to the insurance company in the form of a "mortality and expense" fee that represents the cost associated with the tax-deferred status (layer 2).

Layer 3. If there is a variable life insurance policy involved, there are 3 layers of expense: investment management, the tax-favored portion and the cost of the life insurance. You might rightly wonder if it ever would be worth investing in something that has three layers of expense. This is a very appropriate question to ask. But, the issue is straightforward: it's the same issue that you have in all cost decisions you face. Does the value provided by the three layers of benefits adequately compensate you for the three layers of expense you are incurring?

As a good attorney will often respond: "It depends."

To my mind, there are several circumstances in which paying the costs are justified. In the case of creating a guaranteed stream of income for life like a pension, the two-layered costs are often quite justifiable. Because of the unique tax-free withdrawal features of variable life insurance (e.g., use of money without tax or penalty prior to age 59 ½) there may well be circumstances in which using this three layered expense product makes sense. It all depends on your financial situation and your financial goals.

Summary. In the end, what will determine your financial success relative to accumulation goals is the persistency of regular savings; protection of those assets from taxation as much as possible; prudent and appropriate use of life and disability insurance to keep you from backsliding; and suitable investments at a reasonable cost. That, in its essence, is financial planning for the accumulation phase.

II. CREATING NET WORTH

With diligence and hard work, you will slowly but surely progress from laying the groundwork for success to financial success itself. As savings and investments continue to grow and the safety net of insurances are solidified, you will find yourself transitioning to a more tangible and challenging phase of financial maturity: the active management of your financial assets in support of very significant family goals like college education funding and your own retirement.

As you systematically begin to fill the buckets, you will notice that the numbers start amounting to something. It's slow perhaps at first, but the inexorable forces of continued savings and time will pay off.

There are, of course, several things we can do help accelerate the process. One simple example is to get your money to work harder. Applying a prudent asset allocation plan can help you increase the rate of return on your collection of investments while either reducing your overall risk or keeping it the same.

Likewise, a judicious use of tax favored options or tax advantaged financial products can help blunt the degrading effect of income tax. Without doubt, the use of your employer's retirement plan can go a long way to protecting assets from taxation. And strategic moves like placing your capital gain assets in your taxable account while placing your ordinary income assets in your tax deferred accounts can also help. This strategy is not rocket science; it simply takes advantage of the fact that capital gains taxes currently are capped at 15% while ordinary income tax rates are as high as 35%. Pay the tax on the low end and avoid the tax on the high end.

One of the most common questions I get is whether to take additional savings and apply them to paying down a debt more quickly or to invest the money in additional investments. The good news is that there is no bad answer: any additional savings you do will increase your net worth. Is one approach more efficient than another? Perhaps.

In the case of high interest debt, particularly consumer debt that does not qualify for income tax deductions, I prefer to pay off the debt rather than to invest. So long as the debt is a temporary aberration and not the result of continued overspending on your part. Recall that this process is sequential and if you are consistently overspending then you are still mired in step one. But, if the debt is a one-time occurrence, then I like to pay off the debt and move on.

In the case of a mortgage or other "productive" debt, like a business loan, you may find you are better off continuing to accrue assets by saving and investing. First, we know that if the debt interest is deductible, Uncle Sam is defraying the overall cost. We also know that there is substantial advantage to having the additional assets on your balance sheet. If you pay off the debt, then the capital is sunken. The only way to get it back out is to borrow again, which puts you right back into the debt you were trying to avoid in the first place. Where possible, I would rather see clients build capital in their barrel 2 investments. They can always cash them in and pay off the debt if they want. But, why give away capital unless you absolutely have to.

The final point here is to follow the process. Set up systematic investment programs that help you fill your barrels on a consistent basis. How much you put in each month is not as important as making sure that you make the investment each month. Protect your investments from taxation where possible and be prudent with your debt. And then sit back and watch your net worth grow.

III. MANAGING FINANCIAL SUCCESS

College Planning or Saving for the kids

Apart from health care costs, the fastest growing component of family expenses is education. Whether measured by property tax increases, independent school tuitions or the skyrocketing price tag of college costs, education is an ever increasing portion of family spending. While you may debate the merits and qualities of one college over another, the facts are clear. Children with 4 year college degrees earn, on average, 3 ½ more in lifetime income than those without one.

Therefore, economically painful as it may be, parents continue to bear the cost of higher education in the optimistic view that it is a solid investment in the future. I heartily concur.

The numbers are staggering. For school year 2011-12, tuition and board at Penn State, main campus, is pushing $40,000. High quality, mid-tier schools like Lehigh and Bucknell Universities and the Ivy League head turners are now over $55,000 per year. As one client says, only half-jokingly, "that's a Corvette a year for 4 years. I'm still driving an Accord!"

A. Funding options

There is no getting around the fact that most people need to begin saving for college sooner rather than later. Funding an entire year's tuition from current earnings is unlikely for most people. Often, the stay-at-home parent that raised the kids will re-enter the workforce as the children are going off to high school. The new found income from the second parent at work becomes the "college fund." This is not at all a bad strategy. However, with increasing frequency, I have noticed that the stay-at-home parent stays at home even throughout their kids' high school years. With all the pressures and situations that confront teenagers these days, many parents find it essential that they be home for their children even as they age.

As discussed in the Accumulation Phase, the key to reaching the goal of fully funding a child's education is to start early. Systematic, steady savings and investments that begin when the child is very young are most effective. There are several ways this can be done.

A straightforward approach is to set up a systematic monthly investment program into a series of mutual funds that are growth oriented. If you own them in your own name, you control everything. However, you also get all the income tax that goes with the investment. If you understand the value of tax avoidance in building wealth, you will recognize that this might not be the most effective way to fund education expenses if you are doing this over the 18 year span before your newborn goes off to school.

One option is to use a Uniform Transfer to Minors Act (UTMA) account that allows you to shelter some of the tax. In return for giving up personal access to the funds, you can transfer the tax obligation to your child. The tax advantage arises from the fact that the money is taxed at your child's rate, not yours. However, the trade off is that the money is now officially in your child's name (and *not* yours). You are in control and you are responsible for the funds while your child is a minor, but it is officially their money. It must be spent for their health, education or welfare. Thus, you cannot buy that new Corvette for yourself.

In return for giving up some use of the funds, you are able to shelter the investments in a UTMA account from taxation to the extent that earnings do not exceed an amount that is indexed annually. Currently, the amount is $1,700 per year. The first $850 of earning is entirely tax free in a UTMA and the next $850 is taxed at 15%. Beyond, this however, the excess taxable income is reported and taxed as income to you. In such a case, you have the worst of both worlds: you gave up control of the money *and* you get no tax break. Thus, there is a natural limit to how much one typically should commit to a UTMA account. Roughly speaking, if you have $22,000 earning 8%, that creates $1,760 of taxable income – the UTMA tax ceiling. Above $22,000, a UTMA often fails to deliver significant benefit.

B. 529 Plans

As an incentive to have individuals save for their children's education, Congress authorized the individual states to offer a tax favored investment plan specifically aimed at confronting the education funding issue. As the 401K plan represents the Internal Revenue Code's section which created it, the 529 College Savings Plan references its own section in the Code.

The basic idea is that each state may offer a program which is federally income tax deferred for investments made under a 529 Plan. If the subsequent funds are used for education costs incurred beyond high school education, the funds are entirely tax free. However, if the funds are removed for something other than education, the gains are income taxable and have a 10% penalty attached.

Over the years, plans have added on to the basic design. Depending on the state of issue, the earnings may also be state income tax free. In some states, you may even take a state income tax deduction for contributions made. An excellent source of information on this ever changing landscape is: http://www.SavingForCollege.com.

Despite the fact that each state can offer such a plan, you can use any plan you want. There are no limits based on where you live, where the plan is sponsored, or where your child goes to school. There can often be advantages to using your own state's plan, but those should be balanced against the advantages of other state's plans. For instance, Pennsylvania has one of the weakest plans available; yet, Pennsylvania residents enjoy a state income tax for contributions (to any plan, anywhere) and state tax-free withdrawals (from any plan, anywhere).

Investments are divided into three broad categories. Again, Congress only provided the framework, so interpretations are fairly open. One option is to pre-purchase credits (or their equivalents) through a contribution and deposit system with the state's treasury. For example, if a credit at the sponsoring state's university system is $550 today, then your deposit of $550 "buys" a credit (whatever the eventual cost) for when your child is ready to use it.

This pre-paid tuition plan essentially guarantees that you will always keep pace with inflation since one credit always equals one credit no matter the later cost. However, buyer beware. Since you are "banking" with the state treasury, you are at their mercy. If the state budget is in chaos and funding needs are not met, one might find an "excise tax" or surcharge levied when you go to cash in your credits. This is a real risk.

A second type of investment plan involves a third party money manager, typically a mutual fund company. For example, the ABC Family of Mutual Funds will contract with the state to provide a menu of appropriate investment options. The fund company pays the state a fee for the "privilege" of providing the investment service. You as the investor can then contribute to an account at the fund company and choose from a selected menu of their investment funds. You are in control and again, you take the risk of performance.

The third option is really a variation on the second one. Here, instead of going directly to the fund company, you use a financial advisor who assists you in investment selection, funding levels and servicing questions. As in many aspects of your financial plans, you can go it alone or you can go with a co-pilot. Such plans are sometimes called "advisor sold funds" as opposed to their counterparts which are often referred to as "direct sold."

In all circumstances, a 529 plan account is comprised of 3 actors: the participant, the successor participant and the beneficiary. The "participant" is the person in charge. This person makes all decisions on investments and distributions and is responsible for proper recordkeeping. The account is registered in this person's name with his or her Social Security number attached.

A "successor participant" is named to step into the place of the "participant" if the participant is unwilling or unable to serve. Often, mother and father will play these roles. In the case where a grandparent establishes a 529 plan for a grandchild, the successor is often the child of the participant (and thus the parent of the grandchild).

The entire 529 exercise has been undertaken to benefit a child so it makes sense that the "beneficiary" is the child to whom the money has been allocated. When this child is ready to use the funds, the participant makes a withdrawal on the beneficiary's behalf. It is the beneficiary who must satisfy the "post-secondary education" requirements in order for the withdrawal to be income tax-free.

The beauty of a 529 Plan is that there is a transfer feature that allows for multiple applications of the money within a family. Basically, the participant can transfer money from one beneficiary to another without income or gift tax so long as the new beneficiary is related in a direct way to the former one. "Direct" is meant to cover all siblings and cousins in the same generation as well as all family members up and down the family line. So, mother, father, grandfather, grandmother, future children and siblings are all covered.

A grandparent's gift to one grandchild can be used for *all* grandchildren as well as for their own children even if they are adults. Recall that "post-secondary education" is fairly broad. It can cover graduate school; dental, law, business and medical school; technical school; professional continuing education and more.

The final advantage of a 529 Plan is the special gifting exemptions that go with it. You may already know that each person can gift $13,000 per year to another person without gift tax implications. So, there would be no issue with two grandparents combining their gifts to make a $26,000 contribution to any one grandchild. However, a special exemption allows a 5 year aggregation of gifts which could result in $130,000 of total contributions to any one child or grandchild in one year. A special tax declaration must be made each year, but the tax effect is $0 for such a gift.

III. MANAGING FINANCIAL SUCCESS (continued)

Retirement Planning or Saving for you

A. Introduction

The most wide ranging topic in personal financial planning is retirement planning. The preparation required for this major life accomplishment is substantial. Yet, a majority of recent retirees report that they spent more time planning a two-week vacation than they did planning their entire retirement. Is this really true? I suspect not. But, I do know that the daunting task of envisioning and then planning out one's retirement is a project that is better set to the side while you consider what villa to rent in Tuscany. It's just more fun!

For virtually everyone though, retirement is inevitable. It may come on your terms: you may get to retire when you want, where you want and how you want. But, most people find that retirement becomes a compromise of competing issues – health concerns, family events, work related obstacles, and so on. You will retire and the question will be how much control you end up having over the circumstances.

One way to have more say in your retirement rather than less say is to have the financial wherewithal to cover the contingencies that will inevitably arise. I think you know this intuitively; the more money you have, the more control you have. Almost everybody assumes this to be the case. Yet often, it is the person with the best *expectation* of retirement that can retire more easily – regardless of how much money is involved.

By expectation, I mean the knowledge of what is possible well before the moment arrives. For example, "I'd like to retire at age 62, but could I walk out the door at age 60 if my new boss turns out to be a real jerk?" Or, "I hope to be able to retire full-time at age 65 but what if this medical condition worsens to the point where I have to go part-time?" These are the kind of scenarios and options that must be evaluated well ahead of time in order to be possible. And the better you know your options, the more likely you are to make a better decision. And, the more likely you are to be satisfied with your decision.

With that in mind, let us start with a general overview of retirement planning and then proceed into the more specific aspects of what makes a sensible, flexible retirement plan given the vagaries of 21st century living in the good old United States.

B. Overview

The overall trends in retirement planning are pretty obvious and well reported in many popular media outlets. The baby boomers are entering their retirement years in large numbers and will continue to do so over the next 20 years. Defined benefit plans, or pensions, are being eliminated or frozen at a rapid rate. This means employers are no longer willing to shoulder the long term well-being of their former employees. Instead, 401K plans, or defined contribution (as in, *employee* contribution) plans are exploding.

We read daily of the looming implosion of Social Security. Each year, there are fewer and fewer workers paying into the system while, at the same time, system beneficiaries are growing at a considerable clip each year. Even with "full benefits" being pushed back year by year, the system will fail sometime in the next 20-30 years by most estimates unless benefits are scaled back. This is a real issue for your retirement plan. Can we depend on continued Social Security benefits at the current level? Suffice to say, another pillar of the average American retiree's façade is crumbling: there is a real uncertainty in the level of future retirees' Social Security benefits.

If this weren't enough, add to the mix that the average retiree in this generation is retiring 4 years sooner than in the previous generation; and, that same retiree will live 9-15 years *longer* in retirement than his/her parents did in their retirement. One final zinger: the cost of medical care is skyrocketing relative to all other aspects of our economy. I don't have to tell you who incurs a disproportionate amount of medical costs in our society, but I will. Retirees do.

This may seem to be a pretty bleak picture, and it could be interpreted as such. But, are any trends that are going *in* your favor rather than against it? There are. Most notably, there is a growing body of knowledge about how to plan for retirement and how to manage it financially once you do get there. That's what we'll discuss for the remainder of this chapter.

C. Pensions

The branch of mathematics that analyzes and quantifies economic risk is called actuarial science. Specifically, actuaries look at the impact of risk on the financial well-being of companies like insurance companies. If you have ever met an actuary you know that they tend to be rather intelligent and analytical – and *not* very funny. But, there is joke that reverberates around the actuarial community and it centers on corporate pension plans:

An actuary walks into a bar and meets up with the CFO of a local manufacturing company. Having heard of the recent woes in American manufacturing, the actuary was curious how the company was handling its pension obligations to the corporation's many retirees. The actuary asked, "So, what is your pension strategy?"

Without missing a beat, the CFO answered, "We plan to work our current workers so hard that they drop over within a few years of retirement. The money we save on them can pay the retired workers who we haven't been able to kill off."

Not very funny, is it? Well, I told you actuaries are not very funny people. But, the reason the "joke" persists is that this really is one of the only ways some companies have to preserve the pension they currently provide.

A more humane and often pursued practice is for a company to freeze its current plan and move to a cash balance plan. We have seen this with Verizon and IBM nationally. Although the IBM employees didn't think it was so humane after all. They sued the company over it. Older employees sued for loss of benefits due to the removal of guaranteed incomes in their pension plans. I suspect we will continue to see companies try to reduce their pension obligations to former employees while former employees try to claw back the financial promises that their employers made to them years ago.

As you may have noticed there has been a steady march toward doing away with the pension guarantee. Former employers no longer want the obligation of paying pensions 30 years from now nor are corporations from a bygone era always able to pay current benefits if they happen to end up in bankruptcy. Bethlehem Steel is our most notable local example. With this inexorable trend looming on the horizon, we all must face this question: because you will not have a pension unless you provide one for yourself, what are you doing now to build one for your own retirement?

D. Managing your thoughts

As I earlier noted, retirement planning can be a daunting task. Over the years, we have found that clients are largely unprepared for the challenge of retirement planning not because of laziness or a lack of intelligence but because they simply have never faced these issues before. And, whenever folks are faced with uncertainty, the normal reaction is to sit back and do nothing.

The first step in the process is to actually contemplate your own retirement. Think about what it might look like. At about what age would you like to retire? Or at what age might it be reasonable to assume that you could be retired? Where would you live? What types of activities would you like to be doing?

In the early stages of your thinking, try not to be overly analytic on the number side. Think big and then let the "reality" of your financial situation work its way into the picture slowly, making adjustments as needed. At the outset, I would confine your "economic thoughts" to the big picture realities – what are your sources of income, are they guaranteed, are they protected from the long term effects of inflation, how long can you expect to live in retirement and so on.

For example, realize that inflation, even if it is only 2.5% annually, will force you to have 28% more income 10 years from now just to live the same lifestyle that you do today. In twenty years, your income level will need to be 64% above your current income just to stay even!

It is particularly easy to procrastinate if you think of your retirement being 10 years in the future. Who thinks that far ahead? Most people don't know what they are having for dinner tonight let alone where their career will be in 10 year's time. But, if you were to reframe the question, you might find yourself being more proactive. While it may be true that you have 10 years to retirement, isn't the question really: How are you going to achieve a satisfying and secure retirement with only 240 more paychecks?

E. Managing your assets – Achieving Financial Independence

During the first half of your financial life, what I have identified as "the accumulation period," you will make many choices that will affect your overall retirement plan. You will choose *when* and *how* to save for retirement, *how much* to save and *where* to save and invest. While these choices may be difficult, the good news is that if you make a mistake during the accumulation period, you still have time to learn from these mistakes and to correct them (or at least adjust your plans).

But as you near and then enter retirement, time will appear to narrow. It may even seem to work against you. You will have a variety of choices to make, choices that will affect your finances and your lifestyle in retirement. Among the ones to consider are:

1) What adjustments, if any, should you make to your investments as you approach retirement age?

2) When should you start taking Social Security, and how will it affect your other income sources?

3) What pension option should you choose? A survivor option or a maximum pension?

Obviously, there are numerous others. But, they all have the same quality. As retirement grows closer, you have less time to correct any decision-making errors you make. There will be certain crucial decisions you will undertake that can be catastrophic if done incorrectly. And, once incurred, they cannot be undone. That's why retirement planning with an advisor who specializes in this area is so crucial.

Yes, I know that there are plenty of internet sites and 401K planning software tools and even Turbo Tax and Quick Books add-ons that purport to help you "plan for retirement." My reply is this: "Warning: Wisdom sold separately."

Of course, you would never see this on the website or planning software output page. It's not something the "do-it-yourself" crowd wants to promote too loudly because this is their Achilles Heel. The information coming from TV, radio and the web is all fine and good, but please realize that those sources give people only what they can give: information. They cannot impart what people contemplating retirement so desperately need; what they need is *advice*.

The crucial aspect of retirement planning to recognize is that the strategies you employ and investment choices that you make while you are saving *for* retirement are often very different than the strategies you use and choices you make while preparing to live *in* retirement.

F. Retirement Income Planning

While there is an entire chapter dedicated to the specifics of this topic, the general transition from planning *for* retirement and living *in* retirement hinge on the transition from accumulation planning to distribution, or income, planning.

Generally, the question is: will your plan guarantee that your nest egg won't run out during your retirement years? Realizing that pensions and Social Security are an ever shrinking part of a retiree's income, effective management of personal assets will increasingly be the single most important component that determines the quality (and quantity) of your retirement income. In the next chapter, I will discuss this idea in much greater detail as we explore the issues of reaching financial independence.

Chapter Four

ACHIEVING FINANCIAL INDEPENDENCE, PART I

Retirement Planning

In the previous chapter, I outlined the first three stages of financial maturation for the typical family. Progressing through the stages takes time, patience, and hard work. The payoff for those who are diligent savers and successful investors is the financial freedom that comes with true retirement. By this term I mean a point in your life where you work because you want to, not because you have to.

Where appropriate in this chapter, I will intersperse the psychological components of a good client-advisor relationship with the overall discussion on the mechanics of retirement planning. Obviously, each relationship between retiree and advisor is going to be unique, but there are some issues that appear to be universal. More often than not, however, this chapter will be focused on the eminently practical and most relevant question: will your retirement income outlive you or will you outlive it?

True financial independence arrives at the moment when you honestly believe that you will never need to work again for a paycheck. You can simply have your assets provide the paychecks. Notice that I did not say that financial independence arrives *when* you have enough assets to provide an unending source of income. In my experience, I have found that *when* people have enough money and when they *believe* they have enough money can be years apart. Sometimes decades.

The difference between the reality of actually having enough and believing you have enough introduces us to a part of planning in this stage of financial maturity: the psychological element of money. In recognizing this disconnect between *having* enough money to retire comfortably and *believing* you have enough money, a client and an advisor must communicate on two levels. First, they must discuss and understand the facts of the financial picture and second, they must probe and question the retiree's underlying psychology – i.e., "how are you feeling about your money situation in retirement?"

Of course this question yields several others. How will I handle ever rising medical costs? What are the prospects for long term care needs? Can I keep pace with inflation? Is there a way to guarantee at least the income I need to remain independent? And a host of others.

You should know this from the start: this will be the most challenging section you will read. It is complex and nuanced, and for most people, retirement income planning is a fairly foreign topic. If you want to properly prepare for success in your retirement though, you must master this section.

Preparing for retirement in the general sense is normally centered on determining the critical mass of capital necessary to retire without fear of running out of money. I have called this the Accumulation Phase, the period of time during which you save, invest and try to build up to the critical number.

Once you reach this pinnacle, you should, of course, celebrate. After all, you deserve a celebration for the meaningful work you have done throughout your career. However, this "win" simply entitles you to move on to the next round, kind of like winning the semi-finals at the US Open so you can move on into the finals. In this instance, the finals consist of playing the "retirement income" game: can you make the money last the rest of your life?

You are ready for this challenge when you realize your investment psychology has changed from watching the markets to see how much you might *make* in one day to worrying about how much you might *lose* in one day. The transition from trying to make another dollar to trying to protect the ones you have signals the beginning steps of planning your retirement.

A. The Basics

In your retirement, you can hope to have three types of income:

1) Your essential income – the money that allows you to live at a baseline, comfortable level. It is the "must have" income check each month.

2) Your fun income – the extra income that allows you to really enjoy life:

   playing golf, vacationing, traveling, etc.

3) Your bonus or legacy income – the money that will provide your heirs and your favorite charities with the lifeblood they will need to flourish in the future.

For most people, there is a corresponding list of four income sources to meet these needs:

1) Social Security

2) Employer pension

3) Income from personal assets

4) Continued work

Because you have little or no control over Social Security and pension payments, we consider these relatively fixed income streams. There is some small inflation protection in the Social Security stream, but rarely is there an inflation hedge in the employer pension you may receive. Thus, it should come as no surprise that the ultimate amount and quality of your retirement income will be based on the income you can generate from continuing to work and from your own investment portfolio.

B. Social Security

Your Social Security benefit is somewhat within your control as you have the ability to determine when you begin payments. While I will skip over the specific ins and outs of the Social Security benefit system, I do want to identify a couple of key factors to consider.

Realize that all eligible participants of Social Security begin with a full benefit based on the amount that the participant has contributed, how long the contributions have been made, and on the participant's age. The current wave of retirees will see their full benefit available around age 66. However, you probably already know that you can start your benefit as early as age 62. You will take a reduction in monthly payment for this opportunity, so the question will be: Is the smaller monthly amount that you have available at age 62 worth taking, relative to the larger monthly amount you will get by delaying your decision?

The Social Security Administration has a calculator available on its website (http://www.ssa.gov) to help you determine the "break even" point of this decision. By break even, I mean the point at which the amount you will collect by starting at age 62 will equal the amount you would have collected if you had waited until your "full benefit" age. Roughly speaking, this point arrives around age 79.

So, prior to age 79, you will have been better off collecting sooner rather than later, since you will have more money in your pocket. After, age 79, you will be better off to have waited until your full benefit age. Of course, we know this only in hindsight; when you have to make the decision, you are only in your 60's. But how long you will live is indeed a crucial question.

Because we really do not know how long you will live, there are two other factors that help make the decision. The first has to do with your current work situation. If you are still working full time at age 62 (or anytime longer), there is obviously no reason to even worry about the decision. However, if you are working part-time, there is a threshold level of earned income that triggers a penalty on your Social Security.

If you make more than $14,640 per year, then you will begin to lose Social Security benefits at the rate of $1 of benefit for every $2 of income over the $14,640 limit. So, if you make $15,000 while collecting benefits, you will lose $180 of Social Security benefits ($15,000 income less $14,640 limit = $360 excess. For every $2 over the limit, the penalty is $1, or $180). Once you reach age 66, this threshold limit goes away and you start earning an unlimited amount without jeopardizing any Social Security payment.

The second issue is more of a lifestyle choice than an economic computation. When is the money more valuable to you? (Not in a monetary sense, but from a retirement lifestyle standpoint.) When will you likely best enjoy the money? Is it possible that additional income beginning at age 62 (even if it is less than waiting until age 66) will be truly meaningful to you as a new retiree?

Put another way: Is the money worth more when you are young, relatively healthy and you have things you want to do as a new retiree? Or, is the money more valuable to you when you may be in your 90's? I recall my 95-year-old grandfather living a very pleasant life. He had a garden, a dog, and a place to take walks. That's all he needed. He did not need a bigger Social Security check. In fact, he couldn't even spend his Social Security check every month let alone the pension check he was still receiving.

My point is that the decision on Social Security may be more one of lifestyle than pure economics. No computer program can quantify that difference – only you can.

C. Employer Pension

What was once a basic facet of any retirement plan, the employer pension plan is now an endangered specie. As mentioned in the previous chapter, more and more companies are doing away with their existing defined benefit pension plans, and since many people now work for multiple employers during a career, there is less opportunity to build a sizable (and meaningful) pension benefit from any one company. Anyone 50 and younger can probably operate under the assumption that they will have no pension payment of any significance in their retirement unless they own the company (and therefore run the retirement plan itself) or are a governmental employee.

With that said, employer pensions are still a major component for the long-since-retired, newly retired, and very-soon-to-retire. For the shrinking pool of folks who have a significant vested pension and have not yet retired, there is one very important aspect of the pension that must be analyzed. This concept is known as Pension Maximization.

I think an example will best illustrate the concept. Assume there is an employee of the XYZ Company who is retiring tomorrow. On his last day, he must make a very important decision on his pension. Should he choose option A: take a maximum pension of $3,000 per month for life *or* choose option B: take a reduced pension of $2,700 a month for as long as the employee lives and assure a $2,700 per month payment to his wife should she outlive him.

There are several variations on this theme, but the fundamental issue is the same. Take the maximum you can get for your life alone, or give up some income now so that a benefit could be extended to a surviving spouse? Which option should you choose?

In normal circumstances, most people would like to choose the maximum payment. Who wouldn't? However, after some thought, and a dubious glance or two from a skeptical spouse, most employees choose the latter option. Can you stomach the thought of leaving your spouse with no pension should you meet an untimely demise? More specifically, can your spouse survive economically without your pension benefit should you pre-decease him/her? At the gut level, most people choose option B, and this is understandable.

However, it is often a very poor choice. Here's why. If you think about it, there are only four outcomes relative to this pension question:

1) You die first and your spouse lives a long time after you.

2) You live a long time and pre-decease your spouse within only a few years.

3) You outlive your spouse.

4) You and your spouse die together.

In three out of the four scenarios above, you are better off to take option A. If you take the maximum payment and live a long time, you will have collected a lot of money. Even if you then pre-decease your spouse, you should have accumulated enough funds by that time for him/her to manage the remaining few years he/she outlives you. Obviously, if you pass away together or you outlive your spouse, taking the maximum would have been the smarter choice since he/she will never receive any of the remainder pension benefit anyway.

Even if the odds of the four possible outcomes are equal, you should take option A since the percentages would be 75% in your favor and 25% against. But the odds are *not* equal! They are actually slanted even more in the favor of option A. By far, the most likely scenario is that you both will live a long time and die within a few years of each other. Thus, choosing option B is really a very poor choice…if you can avoid it.

But, "what if"? What if your family is one of the unlucky to have to endure the situation where you die early and your spouse lives a long time? It could, and does happen to some people. Therefore, you must think about protecting against that possibility. By now, you should recognize what the answer might be. When there is a risk of something bad happening to you and you want to guard against it, what do you use? Insurance!

In this case, I refer you back to the chapter on insurance, specifically to the one of the uses of life insurance. Life insurance can protect a pension and the family that depends on that pension for security in retirement.

Inside every pension plan, there is a calculation made that characterizes your pension payment. It is a "lump sum" value or "present value" of the pension payments the company expects to have to make to you over your lifetime. They do not know for sure how long you will live exactly, but they do know "on average" how long you (and all your fellow workers at the company) will live.

Thus, the company sets aside a chunk of money with your name on it. This money is meant to fund the payment of your pension for as long as you live. Let's say in our current example the amount is $500,000. So, the XYZ Company has $500,000 in the pension plan ready to generate payments to you (and your spouse if you wish) when you retire. In our exercise, it is either $3,000 per month to you or $2,700 per month to your household so long as one of you is alive.

Knowing that we would like to take the $3,000 per month and not worry, the appropriate financial planning approach would be to simulate an early death for you and see what the financial impact is on your family. Does it even matter if the $3,000 per month disappears when you do? If it does, how much would your family need to sustain itself without you and your pension?

In essence, we are doing a life insurance analysis recognizing that income (in the form of the pension) leaves the family when you do. Perhaps some substantial inheritance is also lost. Realize you have earned that $500,000 sitting in the pension fund. It has your name on it. You don't control it, but it is yours. The problem is that you can only collect it $3,000 at a time. Basically, you need to live 167 months in order to collect it all. Anything less than that and your family gets cheated.

D. Income from Personal Assets

Here's where the rubber meets the road. The quality of your retirement will most likely be determined by the success of your investment strategy and your portfolio's ability to generate income above and beyond any pension and Social Security payments.

Social Security is steady, but not substantial. It is moderately indexed for inflation, but it does not grow over time in real terms. If you have a company benefit plan, it is highly unlikely to provide a growing income over time. Therefore, the longer you want to live, the more you want to do, and the higher you want your lifestyle to be, the more dependent you will be on how well you handle your investment portfolio before and during your retirement.

The risks are substantial; investment risk, interest rate risk, investment performance sequence risk, inflation risk, and longevity risk are all very real and potentially very damaging to your financial well-being. You must understand them and you must address them in your investment strategy. To do this, let us start with the common types of investments and categorize each by the type of income they create. Fasten your seat belt; this is going to be a bit jarring.

The most speculative and difficult income investment class to predict is made up of CD's, money markets, and fixed rate accounts. That's right!

You read that correctly. The most volatile and uncertain income producers are exactly the set of investments which most people classify as the most conservative and predictable.

This reversal of roles comes from the fact that we are analyzing income and not wealth accumulation. Recall that in the Accumulation Phase, we classified CD's and their kin as conservative because the principal value rarely fluctuates (unless the income is re-invested). The principal is generally protected from loss. In return for principal stability and safety, you have very little chance to gain much.

In the realm of retirement income planning, however, the behavior of principal is secondary. It is the direction and magnitude of income with which we are principally concerned. In the case of CD's, money markets and so on, income fluctuates all the time. The vagaries of the interest rate markets force interest payments to gyrate daily. You have no control over them and they will fluctuate over time.

Since you (and everyone else I know) cannot predict where interest rates will be next year, would you want your income to be held hostage to the uncertainties of the short term interest rate market? I hope not. At the very least, look at the example of a 75-year old with $300,000 in CD's paying 6% today. If she requires $18,000 today to supplement her Social Security and pension, then today she is okay. Her CD's pay the required amount and the current cost of living is covered.

But what will things be like in ten years? For sure, she will not need $18,000 from her CD's. She will need closer to $30,000 from her CD's to have the same level of earning power as she had ten years prior when the CD's paid 6%. The problem is that interest rates would have to have risen to 10% (note that the entire $300,000 principal value has not changed). Of course, this is highly unrealistic. At best, rates have stayed the same and she has lost about 40% of her purchasing power. At worst, rates have dropped to 3% and our widow is now living on 30% of what she really needs. This is exactly the kind of speculation and uncertainty you do not need when you are well into retirement.

The second type of investment class, which has historically been recommended to retirees, is a fixed income class that includes corporate, municipal, and government bonds. In these investments, the monthly income or interest payment is the same every period until the bond matures. If held to maturity, the principal value will also be known since bonds typically mature at par value, a figure known to the investor at the time of purchase. If you plan to hold fixed income investments until maturity, then short term uncertainties in interest rates are irrelevant. You know what you will get every month regardless if rates are going up or down.

There is some merit in fixed income investments for retirement in the sense that they provide reliable, steady income which can be used to provide a consistent paycheck. However, prolonged reliance on these investments will expose you to the same inexorable erosion of purchasing power as the speculative class of CD's does. Using our example from above, a 6% interest payment every year for ten years will lead to about a 40% *reduction* in purchasing power over time – guaranteed! Fixed income options therefore play only a short term role in good income planning.

Fortunately, there is a third investment class which protects against the ravages of inflation. Equity investments in general and dividend paying stocks in particular are the only type of investments that provide predictable and continuously growing income. Not only is this stream of income steady and reliable, it is also inflation proof. See the investment section on equities for a more thorough discussion.

I should add at this point that real estate investments have similar characteristics to the equity investments referenced above. Therefore, rent producing properties that have positive cash flow can be integral parts of an income plan. However, it can be very difficult to turn rental property into ready cash; by its nature, it is illiquid. In addition, a loss of a tenant means an immediate loss of income. Therefore, real estate can be part of but should never be all of your portfolio.

This should strike you as odd at the very least. I have completely turned conventional wisdom on its head. You have always heard that the closer you get to retirement, the more you need to reduce the risk of your investment portfolio by transitioning from equities (stocks) to fixed income (bond) investments. Certainly, as you age through retirement, you should be even more into bonds and less into stocks. Now I am telling you the exact opposite;

I am telling you that you probably need as much in equity investments during retirement as you had when you were accumulating your nest egg.

To be fair, I am advocating that you might need to reconfigure the kinds of equities you own, but you should not be running toward bonds and CD's and the like. You cannot afford to because it's too risky! If you cut and run from equities, the only provider of steady and growing income, you will risk the retirement you have worked so hard to achieve. You must not allow yourself to be drawn into the trap of an over reliance on fixed and speculative income that is inherent in so-called "safe" investments, like CD's, money markets, and bonds.

E. The Planning Process

Clearly, if you wish to enjoy retirement in relative comfort, you must come to understand these various elements of retirement income. Further, you must formulate a prudent strategy for managing and integrating them. As they say at Mission Control, failure is not an option! The decisions you make here may make the difference between being able to leave a real legacy or being financially dependent on your children later in life.

Retirement Planning Life Cycle

	Pre-Retirement Planning	Acclimation and Maturity
Today		
Savings and Accumulation	Transition	Dependency or Legacy?

The most basic issue to wrestle with is the fact that you must continue to invest in retirement to offset the long term effects of inflation. The fact that it costs more to live this year than it did last year is the reality of inflation; things cost more today than they did yesterday. The upshot of this is that you must continue to grow your income every year just to keep even. Not to get wealthier, not to be better off, just to stay even!

As private pensions continue to be phased out and Social Security continues to founder, individuals will need to rely increasingly on themselves and their investments to provide reliable retirement income.

The unfortunate result of this is that the financial risks of a long retirement are shifted squarely onto the shoulders of individual retirees. Where there is risk, there can be failure. Unfortunately, failure in the form of running out of money during your retirement is not an outcome most people are willing to endure.

As in all good planning, we should begin with an assessment of your needs. What kind of income do you need, when do you need it, and how long will you need it? What contingencies should be factored in?

As stated at the beginning of this section, we can generally categorize your income needs into three types:

1) Essential – the absolutely-must-have income that operates your day to day existence. This is the money that keeps you independent.

2) Discretionary – the money that you spend as you wish, when you wish.

3) Legacy or bonus – the extra money that improves the lives of children, grandchildren, and charities

Essential income includes all the monthly bills and annual expenses that keep your life flowing normally: food, clothing, taxes, energy, utilities, etc. These are the items you cannot do without. Consequently, essential income is non-negotiable. You must have it, every month, without fail. It is the money that will determine whether you are able to remain independent from your children or other family members.

Discretionary income makes retirement enjoyable. It's the money you have been planning to spend for years on vacations, golf outings, fine dining, grandchildren, hobbies, and all the other activities that make retirement a real joy. Because these expenditures are, by definition, discretionary, you can control when and how the money is spent. You are entirely in control.

Bonus income is the money that you hope you never need to spend on yourself. I called this legacy income earlier. Assuming that you never need to spend this income on yourself, this will be the money that will make a difference in the lives of your heirs and your favorite charities. Realize, however, that living a long time in retirement raises the risk of long term, chronic medical issues. Quite literally, the things that used to kill us now debilitate us. Thus, we may live many years with costly, chronic medical issues. Whether you remain independent of your family – monetarily and physically – may be entirely dependent on how well you manage this type of income. If you navigate this successfully, you will have legacy income to pass on to the next generation. If not…

The good news is that there are several financial products designed specifically to address each of these needs. The art of good retirement planning in general, and retirement income planning in particular, is to match those products to your specific needs. How well you do this will determine in large part how well you will live through your retirement.

F. Avoiding the Big Mistake

By now, you are beginning to understand that the financial risks involved with retirement in general and retirement income in particular are many-fold. In addition to the investment risks and inflation risks with which you are familiar, there are several new risks that will affect you as you enter into and live through your retirement years. Let's identify those risks and try to pinpoint the planning points that you should be addressing.

Return to some elementary mathematics you learned years ago. One simple idea you learned probably in middle school was that when you reduce a number by a specific percentage, you cannot return to the starting number by increasing the resulting number by the same percentage. If I start at 100 and reduce that by 40%, I get 60. But if I increase 60 by 40%, I arrive at 84. This is a crucial fact when it comes to your money.

The arithmetic of loss requires you to be vigilant in your quest to preserve wealth. Put a different way, it does not so much matter what happens in good years when investment returns are high; it is what happens to your investments in bad years that matters most. For example, a loss of 40% of principal in one year requires a 67% increase the next year just to return to the starting point. Likewise a 33% gain is required to offset a 25% loss, and an 11% gain is required to offset a 10% loss.

This is bad enough in the Accumulation Phase as you try to build wealth, but the real killer happens when you are in the Distribution Phase. The mathematics gets worse and the results are alarming. Assuming that you are withdrawing 5% from your capital each year, a -40% return in one year would require you to make +82% return in the following year just to get back to even. Similarly, a 25% loss suffered while making 5% withdrawals requires a rebound of 43% the following year. Even a modest 10% loss demands a 17.5% return to get back to where you started.

The arithmetic of loss			
		Accumulation	Distribution †
		(no withdrawals)	(5% withdrawal at end of year)
Stock Market decline*	Number of occurrences in past 40 years	Return required to break even	Return required to break even
-5%	46	5.3%	11.1%
-10%	12	11.1%	17.6%
-15%	6	17.6%	25.0%
-20%	5	25.0%	33.3%
-25%	4	33.3%	42.9%
-30%	3	42.9%	53.8%
-35%	2	53.8%	66.7%
-40%	2	66.7%	81.8%

* The unmanaged S&P 500, 1967, with reinvestment of dividends.

† Assumes declines lasted 12 months or less. Source: American Funds "Insights" Winter 2007

The upshot of this mathematical reality is that each and every new retiree is subject to a risk that few have heard of and even fewer understand. "Sequence of investment return risk" is now identified as one of the most important risks to consider when retiring. As in most risks, you may have little control over the outcome, but you can insure against the risk of a bad outcome.

The major risk is that you will suffer a significant loss of principal in the early years of your retirement and never recover. The "crash" of 1987 or the pummeling of technology stocks in the early 2000's are examples of sharp downdrafts in the stock market which are temporary and ultimately only minor blips on the radar screen of long term investors. The brutal financial crisis of 2008-09 knocked up to 30% off every investment class except US Treasuries. Although the markets went down sharply, they eventually worked their way back to their original high points, and then went zooming beyond to record highs (although we are still waiting for that to happen here in 2012). This is the true course of the stock markets since their beginnings.

If you are accumulating wealth during this time, you can wait out these cycles –perhaps even add more investment money when the markets are temporarily "on sale" – and you will ultimately prosper. But if you are in the Distribution Phase, a significant downturn *while* you are withdrawing can spell disaster. The oddest part of this phenomenon is that the risk is entirely about timing. It matters little *how much* you invest or *which* investment you pick, it matters entirely how much you withdraw and when. When you retire and begin consistently to withdraw money from your assets will determine whether the risk runs against you or for you.

The accompanying charts show this in two examples. Larry the Loser and Lucky Loretta begin with the same $100,000 (chart one). Larry experiences investment returns in the opposite order that Loretta does. His first year return is her final year return. His return in year

2 is her return in year 32, and so on. So long as Larry and Loretta are in the Accumulation Phase, the sequence of returns is irrelevant. Both investors will experience the same average return and both will end with the same amount of money at the end of the investment timeframe.

$100,000 Invested, no withdrawals

	Larry the Loser		Lucky Loretta	
Year	Return	Account	Return	Account
1	(17.37%)	$82,630.00	3.00%	$103,000.00
2	(29.72%)	$58,072.36	8.99%	$112,259.70
3	31.55%	$76,394.19	26.38%	$141,873.81
4	19.15%	$91,023.68	(23.37%)	$108,717.90
5	(11.50%)	$80,555.96	(13.04%)	$94,541.09
6	1.06%	$81,409.85	(10.14%)	$84,954.62
7	12.31%	$91,431.41	19.53%	$101,546.26
8	25.77%	$114,993.28	26.67%	$128,628.64
9	(9.73%)	$103,804.43	31.01%	$168,516.39
10	14.76%	$119,125.97	20.26%	$202,657.81
11	17.27%	$139,699.02	34.11%	$271,784.38
12	1.40%	$141,654.81	(1.54%)	$267,598.90
13	26.33%	$178,952.52	7.06%	$286,491.39
14	14.62%	$205,115.38	4.46%	$299,268.90
15	2.03%	$209,279.22	26.31%	$378,006.55
16	12.40%	$235,229.84	(6.56%)	$353,209.32
17	27.25%	$299,329.97	27.25%	$449,458.86
18	(6.56%)	$279,693.93	12.40%	$505,191.76
19	26.31%	$353,281.40	2.03%	$515,447.15
20	4.46%	$369,037.75	14.62%	$590,805.52
21	7.06%	$395,091.82	26.33%	$746,364.62
22	(1.54%)	$389,007.40	1.40%	$756,813.72
23	34.11%	$521,697.83	17.27%	$887,515.45
24	20.26%	$627,393.81	14.76%	$1,018,512.74
25	31.01%	$821,948.63	(9.73%)	$919,411.45
26	26.67%	$1,041,162.33	25.77%	$1,156,343.78
27	19.53%	$1,244,501.33	12.31%	$1,298,689.69
28	(10.14%)	$1,118,308.89	1.06%	$1,312,455.81
29	(13.04%)	$972,481.41	(11.50%)	$1,161,523.39
30	(23.37%)	$745,212.51	19.15%	$1,383,955.12
31	26.38%	$941,799.57	31.55%	$1,820,592.96
32	8.99%	$1,026,467.35	(29.72%)	$1,279,512.73
33	3.00%	$1,057,261.37	(17.37%)	$1,057,261.37

Source: Lincoln Financial

$100,000 Invested, annual withdrawals of 5% ($5,000 in year 1) adjusted for inflation by 3.1% each year thereafter

Year	Larry the Loser Return	Larry the Loser Account	Lucky Loretta Return	Lucky Loretta Account
1	(17.37%)	$77,634.48	3.00%	$98,000.00
2	(29.72%)	$49,407.99	8.99%	$101,659.70
3	31.55%	$59,680.92	26.38%	$123,163.13
4	19.15%	$65,629.33	(23.37%)	$88,905.31
5	(11.50%)	$52,431.25	(13.04%)	$71,660.23
6	1.06%	$47,163.52	(10.14%)	$58,569.91
7	12.31%	$46,963.67	19.53%	$64,001.17
8	25.77%	$52,876.60	26.67%	$74,878.09
9	(9.73%)	$41,438.28	31.01%	$91,713.22
10	14.76%	$40,870.74	20.26%	$103,716.58
11	17.27%	$41,144.44	34.11%	$132,309.88
12	1.40%	$34,725.26	(1.54%)	$123,277.81
13	26.33%	$36,657.31	7.06%	$124,762.94
14	14.62%	$34,580.87	4.46%	$122,896.80
15	2.03%	$27,615.60	26.31%	$147,560.51
16	12.40%	$23,136.11	(6.56%)	$129,977.75
17	27.25%	$21,291.73	27.25%	$157,248.22
18	(6.56%)	$11,493.47	12.40%	$168,346.61
19	26.31%	$5,854.87	2.03%	$163,097.69
20	4.46%	$0.00	14.62%	$178,012.56
21	7.06%	$0.00	26.33%	$215,681.80
22	(1.54%)	$0.00	1.40%	$209,209.66
23	34.11%	$0.00	17.27%	$235,555.11
24	20.26%	$0.00	14.76%	$260,235.51
25	31.01%	$0.00	(9.73%)	$224,510.07
26	26.67%	$0.00	25.77%	$271,648.38
27	19.53%	$0.00	12.31%	$294,026.59
28	(10.14%)	$0.00	1.06%	$285,747.98
29	(13.04%)	$0.00	(11.50%)	$241,126.65
30	(23.37%)	$0.00	19.15%	$275,179.58
31	26.38%	$0.00	31.55%	$349,501.18
32	8.99%	$0.00	(29.72%)	$232,753.94
33	3.00%	$0.00	(17.37%)	$179,053.49

Source: Lincoln Financial

When we introduce withdrawals, however, we encounter the sequence of return risk. If we begin distributions at 5% ($5,000) in year one and increase them annually to keep pace with inflation (3.1%), the results become very different. Loretta prospers and lives a long, full life with no money worries; Larry on the other hand suffers financial ruin. The only difference – and this is important – the *only* difference was the order of their returns. They each used the same investment and received the same average return. The only difference was the order in which they received the annual return.

In a 2006 study by Moshe Milevsky, finance professor and executive director of the IFID Centre in Toronto, the results are even more striking. If you suffer a significant down market in the first decade of your retirement, you are seven times more likely to meet financial ruin – i.e., run out of money – than you are if you suffer the exact same market in the third decade of your retirement.

By now, I suppose this may be getting rather scary. You already know that you must be invested in equities throughout your retirement years in order to have even the slightest chance of growing your income to meet the inexorable demands of inflation. Yet, you now have learned that by being invested in equities throughout your retirement, you are being exposed to yet another risk that, when it goes against you, can ruin you.

Is there a way out? In short, the answer is yes.

F. The Game Has Changed

Interestingly, the products and strategies you used in the Accumulation Phase of your life – the very methods that got you to this point – may now no longer be relevant. In several cases, they may be downright damaging to your future success. The game has changed and the rules are different. Even the finish line is different. From here on, we measure success not by how much wealth you have, but by how much income you can generate in an unending succession of ever higher amounts during your retirement.

The principal financial products in your toolkit will shift from wealth accumulation instruments to the kinds of products that generate the three types of income we mentioned before. Guaranteed income products, like annuities, will supply the bulk of the essential income needs. Bonds and equities, in the form of stocks and mutual funds, should be the major component of your discretionary income needs. Protection products, like long term care insurance and single premium variable life insurance, will provide the risk management necessary to manage the bonus/legacy income need.

In many cases, these products will be new to you, or at least, they will be used in different ways than you used them in the Accumulation Phase. You may be using the Guaranteed Withdrawal Benefit from an annuity, or you may re-allocate your portfolio from growth to value-oriented, dividend paying stocks, or you may need to divert the insurance premium you had used for disability insurance toward long term care insurance. Regardless, some of the rules have changed and you'd better recognize that.

There is a common misconception that folks have. You do not retire on a lump sum of money; you don't just reach the critical mass of capital, cash out everything, and walk away with a wad of cash, living happily ever after. We know by now that people retire on the *income* that a lump sum of capital can produce, not the lump sum itself. Ideally, you should be able to continue to build the value of the lump sum over your retirement years rather than "live off it" thereby running the risk of depleting it.

The all-important questions to raise here are these:

1) How much of your essential income should you insure?

2) Can you afford *not* to guarantee some significant part of your retirement income?

3) Do you want to be able to guarantee the income necessary for your independence?

4) Does your current portfolio protect you from the risks of retirement income planning or does it actually expose you to them?

G. Conclusion

The idea of retirement income is not new. What *is* new is the complexity of confronting today's average retiree's retirement income need. Over the years, I have seen several different approaches implemented to address the income needs of retirees. There are several new methods in development now as most financial institutions are grappling with this concern. It is becoming the dominant issue of the financial planning industry.

In the next chapter, we will explore three of the most frequently used methods for retirement income planning.

Chapter Five

ACHIEVING FINANCIAL INDEPENDENCE, PART II

Retirement Income Generation

In theory, there should be no "magic" in good retirement income planning. The idea should be the same as with any other kind of good financial planning: identify the needs, the risks, and the goals. Quantify the shortfalls, project the surpluses, and apply economic formulas for present value and future cash flow. These are all straightforward mathematical calculations that a computer can run. So why do we feel so uncomfortable with simple internet-based websites that take the basic numbers of our financial life, manipulate them, and then return a graph-filled presentation called "John Doe's Retirement Plan?"

Well, actually there *is* some "magic" involved – and some artfulness too. Most folks are reasonably comfortable with "John Doe's Retirement Plan" as an exercise in and of itself. It is kind of fun to change the variable inputs and re-run the software to produce different scenarios. But of course, that's all those simulations are: scenarios. And these "what if" scenarios are not real.

But what happens when it *is* real? What will you do when the true retirement bell rings signifying that the drills are over and that this is the real thing?

It is natural to expect some anxiety. You *should* be anxious, nervous, or unsettled. In fact, I get worried about the people who don't at least get a little unnerved at the prospect of receiving their last great paycheck.

This is why most people choose to work with a financial planner. While the mathematical models are all important and necessary, they are no substitute for the experience and understanding that a seasoned partner can offer as you enter the final stretch of your financial life. Your planner has been through this situation many, many times before.

Within the retirement planning world, the majority of planners use one of three methods to help their clients plan for retirement income. In my experience, I have found that these models work reasonably well, especially when investment times are good. However, there are several shortfalls to each of the conventionally used methods just as there are significant risks to which each approach is exposed. A growing body of evidence is now converging on a more robust, inclusive (and perhaps even "magical") theory for addressing lifetime retirement income planning for the baby boom generation.

Let's begin with a brief discussion of each of the three most frequently used methods for planning retirement income. Specifically, we will look at the mechanics of each method, and then look at the particular risks and uncertainties that are left unaddressed by each. Finally, we will look at a new theory of income planning that is gaining wider acceptance within the financial planning community.

A. Systematic Withdrawal Plans (SWP)

The simplest method for constructing a retirement income plan is generally called a Systematic Withdrawal Plan, or SWP (pronounced "SWiP"). The idea is simple and elegant: start with a mass of capital that is invested and earning interest, then withdraw a specified dollar amount every year or withdraw a percentage of the total each year that is less than the amount earned by the account, and voila! You have an unending stream of income that emanates from a base of principal that never depletes. Sounds perfect!

In many cases, it is perfect. There are many folks who can live happily using a system like this. At present, about 45-50% of all retirees are using this approach to satisfy their income needs in retirement. And the vast majority of financial institutions have developed significant technology to support this kind of distribution strategy from its investment portfolios.

As an example, a portfolio of mutual funds is particularly well suited to this approach.

A simple example shows why this approach might be appealing. Let's assume we have a teacher preparing to retire. If he taught in the Pennsylvania public schools, our teacher will have access to one of the very best pensions in the United States. Let's say he will get $4,200 per month for the rest of his life. Further, he is entitled to Social Security benefits starting at $1,100 per month and his wife will get $600 per month for her Social Security benefit.

On Day One of his retirement, our teacher friend will have a guaranteed income stream of $5,900 per month. That's $70,800 per year! Now, let's presume that he has done some budgeting and he realizes that he really wants $84,000 per year for his retirement – whether he *needs* this amount is another story. But he *wants* $84,000.

Based on this example, he needs an extra $1,100 per month (or $13,200 per year) to meet his retirement income goal. If he and his wife have accumulated $500,000 of their own savings prior to retirement, this goal is very achievable. In fact, this situation is perfectly suited for a SWP approach. Starting with $500,000 invested at a conservative 4%, his portfolio should produce $20,000 per year in income. This $20,000 is more than adequate to support his need for $13,200. In fact, not only does it supply his supplemental income, but it also adds another $6,800 (the difference between what he earned and what he used) to the pot for next year. In the following year, he would be starting off with a portfolio of $506,800 on which to earn 4%.

In situations where a retiree has a significant, financially strong pension and a Social Security check to boot, a systematic withdrawal plan often works well. As long as the accumulated savings are significant and the supplemental income needs are modest, the simplicity and predictability of a SWP is perfectly adequate.

Of course, one size does not fit all. As mentioned earlier, there is no such thing as a perfect investment, and as you may have guessed, there is no such thing as a perfect retirement income strategy either. There are risks in adopting this strategy and there are clearly situations where a SWP exposes the retiree to the probability of running out of money before they themselves run out. Obviously, these risks must be understood and addressed.

We have already mentioned "sequence of return" risk in the Louie the Loser and Lucky Loretta section in the previous chapter. In essence, this amounts to a timing risk; the "optimal" time to retire and begin to withdraw funds on a regular basis can be a roll of the dice. If you retired and began withdrawing funds in 1996 and rode the wave of the technology boom, you had a much more enjoyable (and profitable) ride than a colleague in similar financial circumstances who started her withdrawals in March of 2000.

There is a more fundamental risk at play as well. The inexorable grinding of inflation against the purchasing power of your income creates a problem no matter what your income situation is. Since it costs more money to live tomorrow than it did today, the income you start drawing from your investments this year will have to be larger next year, and the year after that, and the year after that, and so on. While this may not seem so important, it really is.

Let's look at a common example that many pre-retirees cite as their "income plan". The numbers may be different for each person, but the basic concept is the same. A prospective retiree comes to see me and he states that by his calculations he needs $40,000 per year of income to supplement his and his wife's Social Security. He feels he is in good shape since he has amassed an impressive $500,000 in assets and his 25-year track record of investments has averaged 8% per year. He rightly figures that 8% earned on $500,000 is $40,000 and he therefore has reached his income target.

In the sense that he will be able to generate $40,000 of income in the first year of his retirement, he is correct. But in the broad context of a 20-30 year retirement for him and his wife, however, he is terribly wrong. The chart on the next page shows why: inflation. If our retiree friend does in fact begin withdrawing $40,000 in his first year, he will have withdrawn the entire earnings of his fund. When, in the second year, we adjust for 4% inflation, he must now withdraw $41,600 to live the same way he did in the first year. Because he is withdrawing all the earnings, the principal value does not grow. Therefore, the $41,600 withdrawal in the second year represents *more* than the 8% earnings we assume he will make in that year.

The Ravages of Inflation

YEAR	STARTING CAPITAL	ANNUAL INCOME	REMAINING CAPITAL	GROWTH AT 8%
1	$500,000	$40,000	$460,000	$36,800
2	$496,800	$41,600	$455,200	$36,416
3	$491,616	$43,264	$448,352	$35,868
4	$484,220	$44,995	$439,226	$35,138
5	$474,364	$46,794	$427,569	$34,206
6	$461,775	$48,666	$413,109	$33,049
7	$446,157	$50,613	$395,545	$31,644
8	$427,188	$52,637	$374,551	$29,964
9	$404,515	$54,743	$349,772	$27,982
10	$377,754	$56,932	$320,822	$25,666
11	$346,487	$59,210	$287,278	$22,982
12	$310,260	$61,578	$248,682	$19,895
13	$268,576	$64,041	$204,535	$16,363
14	$220,898	$66,603	$154,295	$12,344
15	$166,638	$69,267	$97,371	$7,790
16	$105,161	$72,038	$33,123	$2,650
17	$35,773	$74,919	($39,146)	($3,132)

Starting with $500,000 and taking $40,000 in annual income, annually indexed at 4%, and growing the remaining principal at 8%, would leave you bankrupt in 17 years.

This example is hypothetical and no specific investment is used. Your results will vary.

What is important to take away is that over time, inflation creates an ever downward cycle that ends in disaster by year 17. Guaranteed! And to spare you added pain and suffering, I did not even factor in income taxes in this example. I'm afraid that the IRS will not be so accommodating. Further still, this example is highly improbable since it assumes that the portfolio will return 8% *every* year. The reality is that portfolios that do return 8% on average over time almost *never* make 8% in a given year. Instead, they make the kinds of returns shown in the Louie and Loretta example in the previous chapter. We have already seen the added vagaries of uncertain annual investment returns.

Clearly, there are some situations which lend themselves well to SWPs and some that are at more risk of failure. In general, sophisticated research using Monte Carlo simulation has shown that a retiree can confidently start an inflation-protected SWP of 4% or less per year provided that he/she stays invested in a prudent portfolio of equities and bonds. There is a high probability of success for the retiree even if the withdrawal lasts for 25-30 years. But "high probability" and "certainty" do not equate in the mind of the average investor.

As is so often the case when it comes to money, retirees are not entirely the cool, calculating people academicians assume. While research shows conclusively that one can maintain a 4% withdrawal rate over time with a very high degree of confidence, individuals do not always feel so confident when it is their retirement on the line. In the meltdown of the markets during 2000-2002, many retirees began to cut back on their withdrawals or eliminated them altogether in response to declining portfolio values. In effect, these retirees let the tail wag the dog; instead of defining the income they could reasonably afford to take and enjoy, they allowed the market's performance to determine their income.

These people essentially let the stock market numbers dictate (and in most cases, significantly curtail) their retirement. How many cruises, excursions to Disney World with grandchildren, vacations, or trips-of-a-lifetime were lost because folks were riveted by the nightly business report or held hostage by the morning paper's stock page? Many, I am sure. Perhaps then, the most important risk that SWPs expose us to is the "psychological" fear of withdrawing funds from our nest egg while watching it shrink –even if only temporarily.

This is a very real fear and one that we cannot take lightly. In fact, it makes a great deal of sense; every experience and every financial skill a newly retired person has garnered to this point is centered on the Accumulation Phase of money. The measuring stick of success has always been the size of the nest egg, not the income it produces. We should naturally expect the retiree to be somewhat unnerved when the size of that nest egg is diminishing in a down market. And why would we expect them to inflict further damage by continuing to withdraw funds as income?

The key to managing this situation – which incidentally, is inevitable at some point in a 25-30 year period of retirement – is therefore one of education, and to be perfectly blunt, hand holding. A good financial planner will be worth his/her weight in gold to you when times like these arise. Your advisor should remind you that feeling the fear is perfectly normal. He/she is likely fearful as well. But the most important thing will be the conviction to not *act* on that fear. Instead, understanding, empathy, and communication will be vital.

What can we conclude from this discussion? I think we can say that in certain circumstances, a SWP income strategy works well. But there are several risks –sequence of return, market timing, inflation and longevity – that must be considered and addressed before making a decision. And as always, a trusted, experienced financial advisor is an integral part in achieving and maintaining financial independence in retirement.

B. Immediate Annuitization

At the very opposite extreme in strategy is a concept based on the unique properties of annuities. In an earlier chapter, I referred to annuities as an insurance based product that most consumers believe is an investment product. In the case of variable annuities, it really is a marriage of an insurance component with an equity investment component. In this case, however, the immediate annuitization approach to income planning is based primarily on fixed annuities issued by insurance companies.

This concept may sound a bit foreign, but I bet you know it well – just by a different name. If I say the word "pension" to you, I suspect you will think of a constant payment that arrives monthly for a proscribed period of time. In the case of most corporate or employer pensions, the timeframe is the retiree's entire life. A pension payment is, in most cases, an annuitization.

While we have looked at the more general case of a "pension" already, in this section we will look at a more specific strategy known as immediate annuitization. From its name you can surmise two things about this strategy; payments begin right away and the payments are fixed for a period of years or, perhaps, a lifetime. And you are right . . . to a point.

First, let us distinguish between a financial product called a "single premium immediate annuity (SPIA)" and the retirement income strategy called immediate annuitization. SPIAs are well-defined financial products offered by insurance companies. Typically, one invests a lump sum of money at a stated interest rate over a stated period of time. For example, a 65 year old male could deposit $100,000 into a SPIA with a reputable insurance company and expect to receive $700 per month for the rest of his life.

On the surface, this might seem appealing. For his $100,000, our prospective investor is getting $8,400 per year, or what appears to be 8.4% annually. Of course, we realize that at the end of the annuity period – when the investor dies – there is no principal left. In essence, the investor's monthly check is partially interest on the initial deposit and partially a return of his principal. If he lives a long time, those $700 per month checks will add up and he will have a successful investment. If he dies prematurely, then his return will likely be less than the original $100,000 with which he started.

If the investor is unsettled by the possibility that he (or his heirs) may receive less than the original starting amount, he can opt to use an annuity that guarantees a monthly payment to him or a beneficiary until all the money is paid out. This is called the "certain option." It means that the money is "certain" to be paid to someone – the investor or his beneficiaries. However, this certainty comes at a price. To guarantee that the money will all be paid back, the monthly payment in our example will drop from $700 per month to about $660 per month. Thus, the cost of certainty is $40 per month.

Alternatively, if the investor is married, he may want to include his spouse in the payment system. Whether our investor dies prematurely or not, there is a very real possibility that his spouse will survive him – in most cases by several years. What happens to her if his payments stop? We have already seen in the discussion on pension planning that a joint annuity payment is sometimes preferable to a single life annuity payment, even if it is lower. The cost to assure that the spouse receives a check as long as she lives, even if it is many years after the investor dies, is rather high. In this case, a joint annuity payout would be $565 or $135 less per month than the single payment based on the life of just the investor.

If you have followed this example, then I hope you have seen some of the risks and concerns associated with an immediate annuitization income strategy. Yes, the income is guaranteed and yes, you cannot outlive it, however, the most obvious concern is that there is a significant loss of control over the asset. Once you deposit the $100,000 into the SPIA, you have given up use of the principal. All you have left is the right to receive it back in monthly increments with interest for as long as you live. And there is no residual value for your heirs beyond the guaranteed return of the unused portion if you elect the "certain" option.

Further, a retiree receiving fixed, monthly income payments is clearly subject to inflation risk. We know that $700 per month today is not worth what $700 per month was worth five years ago, nor will it be as valuable in five years' time. So, the longer you live and the longer you collect, the more you are exposed to an erosion of purchasing power. True, there are some companies that offer a version of these products that includes the cost of living adjustments (COLAs), but they too come at an expense. Instead of getting $700 per month to start, the investor might start at $625 per month with an annual increase of 3%.

With all these issues involved with a SPIA, why would anyone want to use an immediate annuitization strategy? On the surface, annuitization does not seem all that appealing, but if you recall the psychological risk factor of fear we previously identified, you will begin to see the merits of the annuitization framework. What underpinned that fear and what I think motivates people to use the annuitization strategy is the idea of certainty. Knowing that a steady and unending stream of paychecks is coming every month is enormously satisfying and soothing to retirees. In fact, research is finding that retirees with lower, but steady income are more satisfied in retirement than those who have more erratic, albeit higher, incomes.

The most successful uses of immediate annuity strategies involve a laddering approach to annuities. For example, instead of tying up $1,000,000 in an annuity to generate $84,000 a year of income for life, a retiree might prefer to use $400,000 in an annuity that pays $84,000 per year for five years and is then complete. At the same time, take another $400,000 and invest it in a deferred annuity that is earning 5%. When the first annuity runs out, the second one will have grown to roughly $510,000. If one then annuitizes that annuity for five years beginning in the sixth year, it will pay about $107,500 per year for five years.

In addition to keeping more control, the retiree has also created an automatic inflation hedge by increasing his income from $84,000 to $107,500 over five years. And the $200,000 which was never in an annuity has been available for use all along. In fact, if that money had been invested for the ten years at 10%, it would have grown to over $500,000!

In summary, the immediate annuitization approach offers certainty and predictability at the price of control and possibly inheritance. For these reasons, it is most often used by truly middle class retirees who are trying to maximize their long term income without regard to inheritance. Wealthier folks typically use this strategy for a small part of their wealth, perhaps to guarantee their living expenses or to provide a baseline pension for themselves.

C. Guaranteed Minimum Withdrawal Benefits (GMWB)

A relatively new, rapidly growing retirement income strategy is a variation on the annuity ideas presented above. The basic idea is the same, implementing an annuity from an insurance company, but in this version, a variable annuity is used instead.

Because inflation risk is a significant deterrent to using a fixed-annuity-only strategy, the use of a variable annuity (see chapter 2 on Investments and Insurance) addresses the retiree's need to have investment options available that can outpace inflation. The GMWB feature is then added on to the variable annuity as a "rider", or optional benefit. The sub-accounts in the annuity provide the investment vehicle and the rider provides the guaranteed income vehicle. The cost of such a "rider" is considered a "layer 3" expense and ranges from .35% to 1.50%.

While many companies now offer this type of product, each with a unique version, there are some basic, universal concepts to GMWBs. Typically, there is a provision that guarantees a fixed percentage of income from the account. As an example, a common figure is a 5% withdrawal benefit. If you have a $100,000 account with a GMWB of 5%, then you are guaranteed to get $5,000 of income per year from the account.

Some companies will make this promise for a minimum of 20 years. This may sound fine, but it is not really all that exciting. Keep in mind that if you receive $5,000 for 20 years, all you are really getting is a guarantee that all your money will be returned to you over the next 20 years. Other companies will protect the $5,000 payment for life no matter how long you live, even if the true account balance is exhausted before you pass away.

This approach is more appealing in that it guarantees that you will never go without a pay check. In effect, it is a pension – a guaranteed payment for life. But this protection comes with an added benefit that the previous annuitization strategy did not. When you die and the annual payments to you stop, there is not a loss of inheritance. Whatever the baseline investment account had grown to, or whatever was left from your original investment, can go to a beneficiary of your choosing.

If we look at our previous example, we can see this difference in action. Recall that we had $100,000 annuitized over the life of a 65 year old male. He was getting $8,400 per year from his fixed annuity, however, when he died, any remaining balance of the original $100,000 was forfeited. In the current discussion on GMWBs, our retiree would get a guaranteed 5%, or $5,000, per year from his initial $100,000 deposit –obviously less than in the annuitization example. However, if he were to be unceremoniously run over by a bus on his way to cash his first paycheck, his heirs (most likely his spouse) would still get the remaining $95,000. So, there is a trade-off between payout (yearly income) and control (residual value to heirs).

There are several other interesting features about the GMWBs that deal with the risks we identified in the other two strategies. Many GMWBs offer a "step up" in the guaranteed income. At different points in the life of the GMWB investment, the investor has the ability to lock in investment gains if there are any. For example, let's say that our hypothetical investor chose a moderately aggressive portfolio of sub-accounts within his variable annuity, and let's assume that he made 11% in the first year of his investments. At the end of the first year, we would expect his account value to be $105,450 since he would have deposited $100,000, then withdrawn 5% or $5,000, and then made 11% on the resulting $95,000 in the investment pool.

If the annuity company he is using for this investment allows for a "step up" after one year, our investor friend will certainly want to take advantage of this. Here's why: we know already that his GMWB guarantees him a $5,000 pay out next year, so he cannot go any lower than this. But can he go higher?

Well, the step up provides for a "look" at the account value at the end of the first year. If the account value is now $105,450, the question becomes: is this higher than the previous guarantee level of $100,000. Clearly the answer is yes. So, the 5% guarantee in the second year now "steps up" to the new "high water" mark of $105,450. Thus, the guaranteed income in the second year is 5% of that figure, or $5,272.50. Moving forward, this becomes the minimum amount of income *every* year. And it will stay that way until there is another year where the ending balance is greater than $105,450 at which point the step up occurs again.

This basic mechanism makes the GMWB approach very palatable because it addresses some of the major concerns from before. First, it offers a protection against inflation. Second, because the payments never end until death, longevity risk is covered. Many companies even offer their GMWBs with a provision to cover a "joint life," meaning that the payments continue through the lives of husband *and* wife. Third, GMWBs are a type of portfolio insurance. Whereas in the SWP strategy, one's income could be exhausted if market performance was poor; the GMWB approach has a built in guarantee for income even if the underlying investments go to zero!

Is this then the silver bullet solution? Well, not entirely. First, the cost of this program can be high. If we factor in the costs of managing the sub-accounts, the mortality and expense charges of the insurance company, the administrative cost, and the actual cost of the GMWB rider, you may be looking at an overall fee of above 3% per year. Even if the underlying investments make 8% on average, you will make no headway on building your wealth since 3% will go to fees and the remaining 5% you will use for income.

The second concern has to do with the guarantee itself. While it is true that you can take 5% of the principal as a guaranteed income, you cannot take more than that. If you do, then the guaranteed is eroded or eliminated altogether. You would never want to put all of your retirement money into a strategy like this because it would hinder the flexibility of your funds. If our retiree friend wanted $6,000 in his second year instead of the $5,272.50 he was entitled to, he would significantly reduce the guarantee he had worked so hard to get in the first place.

Clearly, then, GMWBs have several advantages to which most retirees would like to have access. However, the limits that come with the guarantee are such that few retirees could comfortably use this strategy will all their retirement money. Is there a better way?

D. Income for Life

In the preceding sections, we have discussed the three most frequently used retirement income strategies. In each case, we have touched on the strengths and weaknesses of the strategy. If our analysis simply stopped here, it would appear that there is no single strategy that can be confidently adopted by any retiree.

In my experience, however, there is a better approach, one that gives all retires a significantly better chance of success. The concept is known by several names and is championed by a number of significant planners and companies in the financial planning industry. My preference is to call this approach *Income for Life*.

You may recall in the discussion on accumulation, I noted that the preponderance of your investment returns (and thus your wealth) is determined by the asset classes in which you are invested; the actual investments themselves are not nearly so important. One blue chip mutual fund is pretty much like all other blue chip mutual funds. But when it comes to the distribution or income phase of life, the tables turn. The investment mix across asset classes begins to diminish in impact as one begins to draw income from a portfolio. In its place, the allocation of income sources and the products that create them become far more important.

In essence, Income for Life is a combination of the three approaches we have outlined above, integrated across a timeline of the retiree's remaining years. It is the process of properly diversifying one's income sources. The uniqueness of the Income for Life strategy hinges on two important insights. The first is that the typical retirement that baby boomers will experience today has three segments: the "go-go," the "slow-go," and the "no-go".

This may sound odd, but I think most people have experienced something like this with family members in older generations. The opening 10-15 years of one's retirement is typically the most active and the most expensive. This is the "go-go" phase. Somewhere in the mid 70's, retirees begin to slow down, either mentally or physically, and they enter the "slow-go" phase. Eventually, retirees realize they have done all the things they wanted to do or they begin to wear down to the point where they enter a "no-go" phase. The upshot of this is that most retirees have 3 different economic phases of retirement spending habits. In the "go-go" phase they are spending at a high rate and require suitable annual "raises" to meet inflation. Then we see a plateauing of spending begin in the "slow-go" phase where their activity is leveling off. Finally, we see a significant drop off in basic spending in the "no-go" phase.

The Income for Life strategy is designed to embrace this changing of spending patterns over time. Just as a well-constructed investment portfolio is meant to combat several risks and uncertainties at once, the Income for Life approach combines the specific income strategies laid out above to address specific risks and concerns related to a broad retirement income plan that has changing spending patterns. The Income for Life strategy pulls together the best of SWPs, immediate annuitization, and GMWBs into a unified strategy that attempts to confront all the financial risks that a 30-year retirement may encounter.

The second important insight that the Income for Life approach embraces is what I will call "buckets of money." This concept is not too dissimilar from the barrels of money I introduced in the Accumulation Phase in Chapter 3. As before, money has a particular use and timeframe over which it will be used. We used the analogy of a barrel in Accumulation Planning as a vessel in which we store important things – fine wine, whiskey or, in this case, your wealth. As we move to retirement income planning (the Distribution Phase), I change the analogy to buckets to connote the idea that we are temporarily storing the money in a bucket until we need to "pour" it out so it can be used.

It is not nearly as crude as it sounds, and besides, it works! In fact, it works really well! Most of my clients may not be able to recite the full extent of their retirement income plan, but they sure do know what "bucket" they are talking about.

The "buckets of money" approach is based on a premise from our previous discussion on asset allocation. We have seen that there are no perfect investments. No one investment can do all things at all times; rather, each investment class performs a specific function that, when aggregated as a portfolio of multiple asset classes, covers all the possible needs a person may have. The "secret" art of retirement income planning is to construct a portfolio (the "buckets of money") that maximizes the probability of success for any given retiree and his/her financial needs. This includes not only the portfolio of investments but also the selection of income generating strategies.

E. The Bucket Brigade

Recall from the section above on Avoiding the Big Mistake that there is a fundamental contradiction in retirement planning. While it appears that every retiree needs to have the bulk of their investments in equities to ward off the inexorable erosion of their purchasing power by inflation, it is also true that a strategy of constant withdrawals from an equity portfolio can end in disaster if the sequence of investment returns runs against you.

The solution to the dilemma is a "bucket theory" of money which addresses the sequence of return risk by avoiding it as much as possible. This may sound a bit simplistic, but it works. How do you avoid the dire consequences of withdrawing money from your equity investments in a down market? Easy. Don't do it. OK, easier said than done, but instead of withdrawing your income from your equity investments, withdraw them from non-equity assets that are *not* subject to sequence of return risk. That's simple enough, right?

We start by carving up your remaining years into segments along a time line using important dates and triggering events as borders (see the Accumulation Phase). For example, if you retire at age 57, we would make the first segment age 57 through age 59 ½, since you might need retirement income starting right away, but you will not have access to your true retirement accounts until age 59 ½. An obvious question is: how will we handle that first 2 ½ year period without access to IRA's and 401K's? I'll come back to this in a moment.

To continue setting up the framework, let's look at the rest of your timeline. Age 60 to 65 would be another good segment to mark off as Medicare begins at age 65 and you may choose to postpone Social Security benefits until that time as well. The next important milestone will be age 70 ½ where you must begin to take distributions from your retirement accounts, even if you do not want to. Most people begin slowing down –either mentally or physically – by age 75 or somewhere in the late 70's. This suggests another good demarcation point. Finally, medical issues and expenses seem to begin to be more prevalent in the mid 80's, so we use that age as another marker.

Using this time line, we begin to map the actual number of dollars you will need to live comfortably in each time frame. While we can talk about and understand lifestyle in today's dollars, we must be cognizant of the inexorable force of inflation that makes things cost more and more over time. We must "inflation proof" our analysis. If it takes $40,000 to live comfortably today, we know it will take about $58,000 to live that well in ten years if inflation runs at 4% per year.

Once we know how much money is required, we do some simple arithmetic to integrate the sources of income you may already have: pension, Social Security, rents, part-time work, etc. From there, we can calculate what shortfalls you have year by year. This is simply the difference between what income you need and what income you will have. This net difference is what your own investments must then provide each year. This is where the concept of "buckets of money" comes from.

In our example, let's assume our new retiree will need $82,000 of his own money to sustain him from age 57 to age 59 1/2. I will admit this isn't very original, but I call this segment "bucket 1." Bucket 1 money will have to be owned outside of any retirement accounts. The age 59 ½ restriction makes it very costly to access retirement money prior to that age and thus, an efficient use of wealth would dictate that funds used from bucket 1 should be non-retirement money. Further, these monies must be certain. We know for sure that we are going to spend this money. Therefore, we cannot put it into any investment vehicle that has principal risk, otherwise there is a possibility that it may be worth less than what we need when the time comes to collect it.

Additionally, we know that the stock market and even the bond market are unreliable over short periods of time. The only prudent investment for money in bucket 1 is a CD, money market, or checking account, preferably with FDIC insurance. The fact that these instruments pay little or no interest is irrelevant. The only thing that matters is that the money is safe and will be there, without fail, to fund the first retirement segment spanning age 57 to age 59 ½.

Note two things here about the investment choice. First, we picked the investment class because of what it does for the income plan, not for what is does as an investment return. The investment return is irrelevant. What matters more is that the money is there to be spent. It does not matter whether a money market pays 1% or 2%. It matters only that the money is protected and available when you need it.

Second, because we know we are going to spend $82,000 in the next 2 ½ years, we need to physically allocate $82,000 into bucket 1. We are going to wall off this money, spend it, and *not* worry about doing so. Why are we not worrying? Because the bucket theory is based on the idea that each bucket of money is attached to a specific timeframe. As you progress along your timeline, a new bucket of money becomes available to spend. It is perfectly OK to use up the whole bucket in each timeframe.

Let's look at bucket 2. We defined the timeframe for bucket 2 as age 60 to age 65. We have three years until we really need the money. Are there any investments you know of that are three to eight years in duration and are relatively certain at providing a fair return? I suspect you do. Remember bonds, be they municipal, corporate or government, are designed exactly for this task. What would be a fair return to assume for bonds over this period of time? Pick a number that is comfortable to you based on your experience. I would be happy with 5.5% for that period of time.

If we calculate that our retiree will need to use $140,000 of his own money to sustain himself for the period ages 60-65, will he really need $140,000 today to do that? The answer is no. Recognize that the $140,000 will be what he needs *then*. What he needs to invest *now*, earning 5.5% is really only about $120,000. This chunk invested today, growing at 5.5%, will grow into the $140,000 he needs when he reaches age 60. So, in bucket 2 we would allocate $120,000 of our new retiree's money into a bond portfolio designed to cover his/her needs in bucket 2.

This process continues throughout the time line as we calculate the amount of money needed to fund each bucket. From our understanding about the nature of equity (stock) investments, we know that as the timeframe of each bucket lengthens, we can assume a higher rate of return on the investments in that bucket. We know that over time, investment returns in stocks are higher and more predictable.

To illustrate this, some perspective may be helpful. In our practice, we regularly use an investment company that has measured 347 distinct ten year histories on its funds. That is, different blocks of ten years across all kinds of investment histories – 1960-1970, 1961-1971, 1962-1972 and so on. In every single case – 347 out of 347 – their investments have returned at least 7.4%. In most cases, the actual returns are closer to 12%. Would it be reasonable then, based on this history, to assume that the money our new retiree puts away in bucket 5, which doesn't start until 18 years from now, will earn at least 8%? I think so.

One of the interesting outcomes of an Income for Life analysis is that the numbers can get pretty big. Do not dismiss them. This *will* be reality for our example retiree and for you. What if our new retiree needs $1,000,000 to protect his lifestyle during the bucket #5 timeframe? This retiree can plan to spend $1,000,000 in his final years of retirement. How much will he have to put away now to assure he will have enough? At 8% return, the bucket will need $250,000 now. At 10% return, the number drops to $180,000.

While the long range numbers are staggering, the reality is that the bucket approach simplifies the strategy and forces you to match up the right investment with the right timeframe. Money in bucket 1 has to be conservative; in terms of immediate need and little requirement for interest, the only answer is a combination of CD's and money markets. But the same is true for bucket 5. The money has to be appropriately invested and invested in a way that gives you the highest probability of success in defending against inflation and longevity risk. The only investments that can do that – the only ones that can make 8 to 10% a year reliably over an 18 year period – are equities. Thus, bucket 5 has to be invested in equities.

The final piece is to aggregate all the buckets and meld them together into an overall asset allocation strategy so that all the money in bucket 1 is available while the other buckets are growing. When we reach the end of the first part of the time line and bucket 1 is empty, we are ready to dip into bucket 2 which has grown into the necessary amount to carry you through timeframe #2. And so on.

This integrated buckets approach answers two major questions facing any potential retiree. Not only can we ascertain whether or not you have enough money to sustain your intended income needs during retirement, the buckets method also defines the retirement income investment plan. It answers the "now that I have enough, what do I do with it?" question.

Obviously, it would be better to know the answer to these questions sooner rather than later. Wouldn't you want to know your probability of success *before* you retire rather than 5 or 10 years into your retirement? So, normally we begin this process with pre-retirees between one and three years before they actually plan on retiring. Naturally, as the retiree's ideas about retirement progress, the plan is adjusted and updated accordingly. Nonetheless, the mid-50's is always a good time to start seriously planning for retirement. From there, we recommend annual reviews at the very least to assure that we are up to date on income needs and investment performance.

F. Overflowing Buckets

Ideally, you will go through the income planning exercise prior to retiring and find that you have some surplus, an amount of capital above and beyond the baseline needs and personal desires that come with being retired. Anything over a 20% surplus is very comforting. Reaching this point signals that you are ready to plan your legacy, or bonus income.

While it is very tempting to start thinking about what to do with a potentially large surplus of assets, most folks are typically pretty cautious. They prefer to live within their means and keep that surplus "just in case." In fact, I find that the people who make it to retirement successfully have *always* lived within their means. So much so, that they cannot make themselves spend more even if they had to. The habit of being frugal and prudent is now in their blood and it does not wash away easily.

But, there does come a time for those fortunate people when they realize that they really *do* have enough money. They will not run out no matter what they spend (within their normal lifestyle spending habits). Someone who has never earned more than $80,000 a year is not going to suddenly develop a $250,000 a year mindset just because they retire.

What *is* more likely is that that new retiree might want to spend $90,000 in one special year of retirement – a special anniversary trip, a family cruise, a vacation rental that allows family and friends to visit for an extended period, or an indulgence of art or collecting. There will be times and opportunities to spend above and beyond your "normal" income and the question will be: can you do it?

A success story. One of my favorite stories is of a client who worked for 38 years at AT&T and was hoping to retire. He had modest needs, a frugal lifestyle, and a lifelong desire to go to Alaska. He wanted to fly to Vancouver, cruise the inside passage, spend time in Denali National Park, and go fishing. The trip was going to cost about $15,000.

Keep in mind that this fellow never made more than $60,000 in a year, only once ever paid more than $15,000 for a car, and his first home cost only $29,000. This was a big deal! It was a lifelong dream, but it was going to cost him a boatload. What to do? Could he afford it?

Certainly by the prudent standards of spending and living within his means, the answer would be no. This $15,000 cost would break the annual budget for sure. He was convinced he would never be able to take this trip until we went through the buckets of money analysis.

What he found was that not only did he have the money to take the trip, he had so much money that his annual income in retirement would be about 20% higher than his current income. Because he was so focused on earning and saving, he never realized that he would be making more money retired than he ever did while working.

Incidentally, he took the trip with his wife, and he loved it! In fact, he has been taking cruises and other trips every year since. His next big adventure is Russia!

So, a properly planned and executed retirement income plan allows you to confidently spend money now *and* later. Spend the money that you want and need to spend to enjoy your early years of retirement without the worry and fear of bankrupting yourself later.

If you are one of the fortunate few who reach that stage in life where you have comfortably more than you need, you will eventually have another question to answer: what do I do with the surplus? Or, put differently, how do I best use the excess wealth that I will probably never need for my own income purposes?

You can always choose to do nothing. In such a case, the money you have spent a lifetime creating will dissipate into a maze of legal fees to settle your estate, including income and estate taxes payable to your favorite

Uncle, and eventually by inheritances to those named in your will. Most of our clients are not predisposed to this unseemly end to their wealth. If they have toiled to create wealth they are not going to allow one final hurdle to deter them from planning out the final disposition of their assets.

There are several areas of planning where these forward thinking people focus their attention. As we discussed in the insurance section, long term care insurance is one area in which folks can deploy their excess income to protect the principal value of their estate from being depleted by a long term, chronic medical situation. Excess annual income can be used to purchase insurance that protects against a catastrophic financial loss due to prolonged need for medical care. Alternatively, some policies can be purchased with a one-time contribution of excess assets rather than by endless premium payments.

Making gifts and contributions of excess income or assets to family and charitable organizations is also a popular choice. When we give funds to our children and grandchildren while we are living, not only do they benefit, but we get the additional joy of watching them enjoy the gift. Whether for education, medical expenses, a new home, or a start-up business, gifts of wealth within the family can strengthen the family bond and help instill your values and ethics into the nurturing of the next generations. Likewise, gifts to the charities and community organizations that have played an important part in your life can be as vital to the charity as they are rewarding to you.

G. Summary

The long road through a modern day retirement is filled with uncertainties. Few people have real experience with handling money over a thirty year period without a paycheck. Creating a sustainable income stream that can withstand the risks of longevity, investment markets, and inflation is no easy task. With the assistance of an experienced financial planner, however, you will have access to the financial products and strategies that give you the best chance of success. The income strategy best suited to you will be determined by your own financial situation and your own attitudes toward money. Regardless of which strategies you use, one thing is clear: retirees managing their finances in the 21st century will endure challenges unlike any that previous generations have faced. A crucial part of their success will be a well-designed and executed retirement income plan.

Chapter Six

INSPIRED LIFE, INSPIRED LEGACY, OR ESTATE PLANNING TO DIE FOR

The three most dreaded words in the language of personal finance are Death, Taxes, and Insurance. And guess what? That's exactly what estate planning is all about. Like it or not, that's what we are going to talk about in this section.

No one particularly likes to talk about dying, but let's face it: at some point you realize you are playing the back 9. You may not know if you are teeing off on #10 or if you are finishing up on #18, but you are definitely "heading for home." We may never really know what hole we're on, but there comes a time when we realize that we'll be "putting out" sooner rather than later.

It is therefore vital to be prepared with a good estate plan before you reach the final hole. Quite possibly, the most expensive day of your life is the day you die. Your family and friends will be shocked enough by your death, there's no sense in letting them later find out that you were woefully unprepared for it. A well-executed estate plan will likely be the last memorable act you perform, even if orchestrated from the grave.

Keeping in mind that it is very likely you will not use all your assets during your lifetime, the basic question of estate planning is: who should get your wealth when you are no longer around to enjoy it? Chances are you already have a pretty good idea what you want to do. It's just a matter of getting your affairs in order so things go the way you want them to.

I. GETTING STARTED

Thorough estate planning begins with the careful consideration of the four possible life outcomes. When you really think about it, these are the only four possible scenarios in your economic life: you are healthy and you cruise into retirement living to normal life expectancy, you are really healthy and you live a long time (longer than life expectancy), you are not healthy and you become incapacitated at some point, or you are really unhealthy and you die tomorrow. I admit this is a little over exaggerated, but the idea is right. The major questions to consider in estate planning are:

1) What if I live?

2) What if I live too long?

3) What if I become incapacitated?

4) What if I die?

It's hard to imagine many folks in their 20's worrying about such things. With the exception of considering the possibility of personal disability, most young people have little financial responsibility – particularly to others. Their need for estate planning is minimal, however, as they mature and assume more financial responsibilities like a home, a spouse, and children, the basic questions of estate planning become important. While I find most people getting serious about estate planning in their 60's and 70's, the truth is that one should begin basic estate planning much earlier in life. For young families, it is never too early to confront the questions of incapacitation and premature death.

Before we start considering each of the four scenarios individually, I find it very helpful to start by writing down what is important to you about money; what it does for you, maybe what it *can't* do for you, what its promise is, what it says about who you are as a person, and so on. This is the personal legacy that goes with the economic legacy that you will leave. You should focus on what is important to you, not what your assets are worth. Think about whether your assets represent education, charity, security, or something else. What is it about money that is most meaningful to you?

The next step is to categorize these convictions based on the four scenarios above. In essence, map out how you want your affairs to be handled if and when you enter any one of these phases of economic life. What do you foresee as the significant financial, legal, and medical dimensions of a major life event? Write down your thoughts and discuss them with your spouse and even your children if you think they are ready for such a discussion.

Now that you have put your priorities down, you are ready to think about the economic value of your assets. Asset ownership typically has five ingredients:

1) the value of current income – e.g. dividends and interest

2) the current market value – what you could receive if you sold today

3) the value of future income – e. g., the future rents from a business property

4) the potential future appreciation – e. g., the future value of a business interest or investment

5) control – in this context, the value lies in who owns the asset and who has the ability to disburse it and to whom.

Assign a value to each asset subtracting any liability or debt from the market value. Rank each asset in order of importance to you using economic value as a starting point, but then adjusting it for priorities of control, income flow, etc. Once ranked, think about each asset and who should inherit it, if anyone. Is it more important to give the asset outright, or is it better to give the future stream of income annually and protect the principal in trust? Is control of the asset important? How much of your estate do you actually want to leave to your family in the first place? How much, if any, do you want to give to charity?

For large estates, say above $2 million, we call this Family Wealth Counseling. It is the controlled exercise of deciding who gets what, when, and how much. When done properly with an accomplished team of advisers, plans often work well and familial harmony is maintained. When done improperly, or more likely, when not planned at all, the biggest heir often turns out to be the IRS.

THE ESTATE PLANNING PROCESS

I. TAKING INVENTORY

- Summarize assets, liabilities, employee benefits and life insurance

- Assign a fair market value to each item

- State clearly the owner, the beneficiary and the insured

II. ASK PENETRATING QUESTIONS

- Who should run your affairs (financial, legal, medical) if you cannot?

- Who should receive your wealth when you no longer need it?

- Do you have any special bequests to family, friends or charities?

- Do you want a corporate Trustee or a family member to preside as Trustee?

  Should you have co-Trustees?

- Who should bear responsibility for investments, insurances, disbursements, etc. when you no longer wish to

III. FORM A STRATEGY

- Ask a trusted advisor to recommend professionals (CPA, Attorney, Financial Planner, insurance agent, etc.) to work on your team

- Designate a team "captain" to coordinate work with all other members

- Examine estate planning options

- Consider the issues: ease of management, cost of implementing, cost of *not* implementing, tax liabilities

IV. DESIGN A GAMEPLAN AND IMPLEMENT IT

- Decide on a plan and put it into motion!

    - Execute legal documents

- Re-title property

- Reposition investments/insurance

- Coordinate beneficiaries

- Notify all parties responsible for your Plan

- Involve one or two key beneficiaries to carry out your intentions

- Review annually

For families where optimal wealth transfer is most important, we use a Maximum Wealth Control approach to planning. After going through the Family Wealth Counseling exercise, we begin to take on the challenge of maximizing transfer wealth by assessing the extent of the estate. Specifically, we need to know how the IRS treats each item. We then assess the potential tax liability of each asset and discuss options for reducing or eliminating the tax liability for each asset.

II. ASSEMBLING THE TEAM

There is no specific formula for determining your estate planning team. Clearly, the more complex your situation, the more team members you may need. At the very least, there should be three essential players: a CPA, an experienced attorney, and a financial planner who each specialize in estate planning.

For attorneys, an advertisement of "doing wills and trusts" is not a sufficient level of sophistication to do real estate planning. One needs to seek out a true estate attorney who works primarily (maybe only exclusively) with estate planning clients. In the financial planning world, there are several professional designations that advisors earn through continuing education and accredited study programs. An Accredited Estate Planner (AEP) and a Certified Financial Planner (CFP) are two such designations that are reflective of significant knowledge and experience in estate planning. Seek out candidates who have these credentials. Further information and background can also be found by communicating with your local chapter of the National Association of Estate Planners and Councils (www.naepc.org).

Depending on the extent of your estate and the desires you have for it, you may need other experts to provide specialized services. For instance, when life insurance is indicated in the estate plan, you should seek out an agent or broker who is a Chartered Life Underwriter (CLU), the premier designation of experience and knowledge in the insurance industry. Likewise, there are several well respected designations in other important areas such as elder law, business valuation, trust operations, and charitable giving. Professionals who work in these special areas are very amenable to working within the estate planning team framework.

As an individual trying to understand and navigate the estate planning world, it may seem overwhelming to assemble such a group of experts. The good news is that you should not have to. All you really need to do is identify one adviser – be it your CPA, attorney, or financial planner – who will act as "general manager." Choose the person with whom you are most comfortable, the one with whom you have the best rapport and the most shared trust. This person can help you assess your overall estate and begin to assemble the team for you. Where possible, your existing advisers should be included as part of the team, so long as they provide the requisite skill and knowledge to meet the tasks at hand. When such people are unable to provide the necessary level of expertise, the "manager" needs to take the lead and bring together the necessary talent to fulfill the estate planning mission. At all times, you should retain "veto" power over who ultimately is on your team.

Typically, the core group of advisers will meet with the client to assess the estate situation and to clarify the client's goals. It is customary for each adviser to spell out specific concerns and areas of opportunity that he/she observes. At the end of the meeting, the "manager" is charged with the responsibility of summarizing the discussion, appointing tasks to each adviser, centralizing communication with the client, and where appropriate, recruiting additional advisers that may be needed to provide special expertise.

As the process moves forward, the individual advisers may work directly with the client to address specific issues, but this should be done with constant communication through the "manager" who is ultimately responsible for directing the entire process. At the very least, the core team should meet annually, either in person or by conference call, to review the plan and verify that it is still in keeping with the client's wishes.

III. THE BASICS OF WEALTH TRANSFER

Now that you know the basic format of the estate planning team and its process, it will be helpful to know what you are going to be discussing with these folks. Your CPA is going to be well versed on relevant advice concerning your personal business and tax issues. The estate attorney is going to be tuned into the possibilities of structure: trust ownership versus personal ownership of assets or alternative business entities such as LLCs or Family Limited Partnerships. The financial adviser should be approaching the conversation from the standpoint of execution. These considerations include what accounts will be used, what investments will be made, how to structure insurance products, and so on.

As a group, the advisers will also discuss possibilities and opportunities for planning. Further discussions should include more sophisticated topics like how are you going to pay the unavoidable estate taxes without wrecking the estate plan? What are the specific liquidity issues that arise from the IRS's rule that estate taxes must be paid within nine months of death? What, if anything, are you willing to do to replace or redirect wealth that will be inevitably lost to the IRS? Does charitable giving make more sense while you are still living or after your death?

These are the important questions that a team of advisers can help you assess and work through. Once you have done this, the final step of the process is easy, and yet, oddly, this is where most plans fail. Often, people go through the difficult task of meeting with their advisers, thinking about what they want to do, and formulating a plan to accomplish the task, yet just as they are about to reach the end successfully, they stop.

Executing the estate plan is actually the simplest part, but many people never follow through and complete the task. Once you have planned it all out, you *must* follow through with signing the legal documents, changing or updating the beneficiaries, changing the title on assets, etc. Without this final, vital step, the plan is for naught.

IV. WILLS

Let me be blunt on the topic of wills; you need one. You *must* have one! In fact, whether you know it or not, you already have one. Your state of residence has a written will sitting on the shelves for every person who dies without having written a will for themselves. It's called the "intestate will" and you *do not* want this will.

First of all, the state written will does not often make a lot of sense. In some states, it gives money to your parents when most likely you would like it to go to your children. Second, by allowing the state to dictate the distribution of your estate, you have lost most of the important tax savings mechanisms available to planned estates.

The bottom line is that you should have a will drawn up and notarized. A competent attorney can draft a personalized, simple will at a reasonable price. This official act tells the world that you have made an affirmative action toward the disposing of your assets upon your death. This should be obvious and straightforward, yet not everyone gets around to doing it. If for no other reason, please make a will to name a guardian for your minor children. Without this provision, your children may end up in orphan's court, even if there is an obvious, ready-and-willing, and loving family member to step into the void that your untimely death would create. Without a definitive statement from you in a will, the courts will decide who cares for your children – not you.

Many of our clients like to go beyond the simple idea of completing a will. In addition to leaving a physical legacy of their assets, some folks like to leave an oral or written legacy of their thoughts, dreams, pearls of wisdom, or advice for the next generation. Often, they do this through an Ethical Will.

An Ethical Will is not a legal document; it holds no legal standing whatsoever. But the power and meaningfulness of an Ethical Will can be one of the most treasured gifts you leave behind. It tells your family what is important to you, what lessons you have learned, and what hopes and dreams you have for generations to follow. It is your moral and personal legacy to those who will follow you on this earth.

The folks who have done this exercise for themselves – whether by writing it down, recording it on tape, or by videoing it – have found it to be very satisfying. The families that inherit these gems cherish them forever.

V. HEIRS

One would normally think that identifying one's heirs is a no-brainer. People who have no money to leave to their kids automatically assume that people who *do* have wealth will leave everything to their children. Frankly, I have found this not to be the case.

There are a host of reasons why; your reasons can be anything you want. After all, *it is your money!* You need not justify your decisions to anyone other than yourself. But, please, make sure you *do* discuss your ideas and your decision with your estate team. Heirs and beneficiaries can be changed over time. What makes sense for your family today may not make sense ten years from now, so be flexible and forward thinking. Your choice of heirs and the methods by which you impart your estate to them will be an important part of your financial legacy.

Children and grandchildren generally do not do well dividing up resources and managing things without a good game plan from Mom and Dad or Grandma and Grandpa. They just don't. Unless you have spoken with them at great length, over a long period of time and in some significant detail about what you really want to happen with your wealth at your death, things will go awry. Human nature and family dynamics often exert odd and sometimes ruinous pressures on unplanned estates.

Talk to your children about what you want to have happen. Ask them what they want or need. You do not have to heed them or appease their demands, but be open about your feelings and open to new ideas so that all the issues can be communicated clearly. The most effective estate plans are the ones that have been in discussion and refinement for many years.

VI. GIFTING

As straightforward as gifting may seem, I am always amused at how confusing it can become for many folks. Simple gifting for birthdays, graduations, or wedding gifts is easy; write a check and you are done. But when it comes to larger gifts, like a new home, things appear more confusing. One basic misconception is that the person receiving the gift may have to bear a tax. Not so! The *giver* of the gift may have to bear a tax – although very often the tax is 0%. Let's look at the basic tenets of giving larger gifts.

Each person in 2012 can give any other person up to $13,000 a year without any issue. The exception is when you "gift" to your spouse, where the gift possibility is unlimited. Spouses can give money back and forth without issue so long as it is not an IRA or retirement account. As a couple, husband and wife can give $26,000 to any one person in a year. Thus, Mom and Dad can give $52,000 to their married children since Mom can give $13,000 to her child and her in-law and Dad can do the same. Factor in two grandchildren in the family and now the gift is multiplied to $104,000 with no tax.

Now, what if Mom and Dad want to give $50,000 to their single daughter? Is there a tax? Technically, the answer is yes, however, in practice, the tax will be $0. Sound odd? Here's why. We already know that Mom and Dad can give $26,000 tax-free under the $13,000 annual gift rule, but since we are $24,000 over that figure, the additional amount must be declared as a "taxable gift" under the estate and gift tax rule (IRS Form 709).

Recall, though, that each person is allowed to give away, under current rules, $5 million estate tax-free. If you are confused at this point, it is important to realize that each person is allowed to give $13,000 a year per person PLUS their lifetime amount of $5 million. So, when you write a check for $5,000 to your grandson for graduation, you are using up your $13,000 annual gift amount, but not your $5 million lifetime amount. Only when you exceed the $13,000 amount do you begin to "eat" into the $5 million lifetime amount.

Now, back to our example of the worthy daughter. The first $26,000 goes toward the annual gift at $0 tax; Mom gifts $13,000 and Dad gifts $13,000. The $24,000 excess gift can be split into $12,000 increments for Mom and for Dad and applied to each of their $5 million lifetime exemptions. By doing this, the excess $24,000 is counted against the $5 million lifetime amount reducing it to $4,988,000 for Mom and the same for Dad. Thus, we preserve as much gift as we can for each. Even though we have reduced the lifetime figure, we are still operating in a zero estate tax zone and therefore, the $50,000 gift is in fact tax-free.

As a caution, whenever you are considering gifts of this size, you should consult your planning team as they will need to file the appropriate forms with the IRS at the very least. It may be the case that there are other more efficient ways to give the gift.

An additional word on gifting has to do with the 529 plans we discussed in the Education section. Any contribution you make to a 529 plan which is not destined for an account that has you as the beneficiary is a gift. If you contribute to an account for your children or grandchildren, even if you are the participant, you are making a gift and you are subject to the gifting rules discussed above. However, 529 plans have a special circumstance that allows you to "super charge" the gift without being subject to the gifting issue mentioned above.

Within the 529 plan rules, any person can make a five year forward gift without having estate or gift tax applied. In essence, a grandparent can give five times $13,000 or $65,000 to a grandchild's 529 plan in one year. The gift is considered a five year gift and is reported as one $13,000 gift each year for the next five years. Thus, the gift applies only to the annual gift amount of $13,000 and not toward the $5 million lifetime amount. The beauty of this is that a large amount of principal goes to work tax-free in the account and no money goes to Uncle Sam. Further, such a gift reduces the portion of the donor's estate that might otherwise be subject to estate taxes.

VII. PROBATE

I have found that "probate" is one of the most feared terms in estate planning. Most clients have been persuaded that probate is the most horrible thing next to Ex-Lax-laced chili. Normally, it is not. Yes, there are some costs associated with probate, and yes, some attorneys draw out the process solely for their own financial reward, but ethical, competent attorneys can use it to your favor. At the very least, avoiding probate is no reason to get stuck into doing the potentially phony estate planning hyped by Living Trust salespeople. More on Living Trusts later.

VIII. POWER of ATTORNEY

There may come a time in your life when you will not be able to speak for yourself. There may be a medical situation, however temporary, that could prevent you from being able to transact financial business. Or, you could simply be out of the country on vacation or on business. In any case, a Power of Attorney (POA) allows someone you have designated to act on your behalf in financial matters.

If the situation is temporary, a basic POA will suffice, however, if you wish to cover a situation where your inability to act on your own behalf is more permanent (a major medical event for example), then you should consider a Durable POA. Such a document is "durable" in the event of your incapacity and would be recognized as a valid legal instrument, whereas a basic POA becomes null and void at the assignor's incapacity.

IX. TRUSTS

As in most planning concepts, a competent team of advisors, including an estate attorney, an accountant, and a financial advisor, is your best source of information on trusts. This book is only really intended to provide basic ideas and concepts on the topic. As such, there is no way I could possibly do justice to trusts here. Nevertheless, I hope the basics will suffice.

A trust starts off as a document that establishes a legal entity known as a Trust. If this sounds odd, it is. The "trust document" – the paper that you sign – creates a legal entity that then stands as a unique "being" until it is dissolved either by the creator or by an expiration of a specified timetable.

Not always, but in most cases, a trust is executed in estate planning to handle the Four Horsemen of the Estate Planning Apocalypse: Creditors, Predators, Outlaws, and In-Laws. I am being a bit flippant here, but the idea is solid. Trusts are meant to protect against creditors who would take your assets against your wishes, against predators who could "dupe" and manipulate your heirs, against your former in-laws in the case of divorce or business disputes, and against current in-laws in the case of future action against your heirs.

In all instances, a trust has at least one Trustee. Most of our clients prefer to have their most personal issues overseen by a trusted member of the family who knows the family dynamics. However, it is often difficult to choose such a person who is competent, strong of character, and willing to act as Trustee. There are responsibilities and commitments that a Trustee must take on now and in the future. These responsibilities and commitments last as long as the trust does. Consequently, it is often difficult for a Trust creator to make the decision to "burden' a family member, no matter how strong a person, to be a lone Trustee (see the appendix for Considerations for an Individual Trustee which outlines the role of a trustee).

Thus, many of our clients prefer to add a corporate trustee as a co-trustee. In this capacity, the corporate Trustee is expected to handle all the technical, tax, and administrative tasks, and bear the fiduciary liability. In tandem then, the family member carries out the wishes of the trust maker while the corporate co-trustee takes responsibility for the details.

Frequently, a trusted family member is named the Power Of Attorney (POA) and executor of the will while a corporate trustee is named to invest, make the appropriate tax filings and, when absolutely necessary, referee difficult family situations. As mentioned above, the POA is a legal document that appoints someone to speak for you when you cannot.

As cited earlier, there are four phases of your economic life to manage from here on. From the standpoint of legal intervention by another party on your behalf, the situations look like this:

1) While you have your health and your wits, you run the show. No need for anyone's assistance.

2) If you live a long time and simply need some help to run the show along the way, you can delegate a family member to assist you.

3) If you become incapacitated, either permanently or temporarily, your business and financial affairs can continue to be managed by someone looking out for your best interest.

4) When you die, your wishes can be carried out.

In the case of situation one, you need nothing more than your own signature to conduct business. A well drafted general POA handles situation number two. A Durable Power Of Attorney is useful in either circumstance two or three, but a Revocable Living Trust (RLT) handles all four circumstances.

If you have followed this discussion, you may now find yourself asking why I rebuffed RLTs earlier only to now appear to advocate for them. Good question. RLTs have mostly a bad reputation in the popular press because they are over marketed. In fact, just as puppies can be "milled", there is a phenomenon called "RLT mills" where unscrupulous attorneys churn out "customized" trusts sold by salespeople who do not know anything about you or the estate planning they promise to provide. These firms are out there and they are the ones that sully the concept of a Living Trust.

As in anything, RLT's are neither the silver bullet solution to everything nor are they the pariah of the journalistic tirades one occasionally sees in the local or national press. They are simply an instrument that, when used properly, can offer excellent options for a client who has particular needs and goals.

Where I find RLT's to make the most sense is when you have an elderly family member who does not have a competent spouse to act on his/her behalf. In most cases, a competent spouse is more than capable of handling matters for a couple without resorting to an RLT. But whether by widowing or by mental infirmity, when a person loses their competent spouse, an RLT begins to make sense for a variety of reasons. Simplicity, ease of management, and avoidance of multiple probates (ownership of real property in multiple states, like a beach house in one state and a primary residence in another, triggers multiple probates) are reasons for considering the RLT option.

One other important trust to be aware of is an Irrevocable Life Insurance Trust (ILIT). In a nutshell, an ILIT is a trust that owns life insurance on you and/or your spouse. It is also the beneficiary of the insurance. When properly constructed, the insurance proceeds are *not* in your estate (for tax purposes), yet the full death benefit remains available for use by your surviving spouse, your children, and your grandchildren.

X. THE TAX SITUATION or COUNTING THE DEAD

To understand the true value of your assets in the estate planning process, you need to understand the basics of taxation. Understand that there is a part of your business or a part of your portfolio that you don't really own. For virtually all people of means, there is an estate tax, an inheritance tax, and some income tax liability that is really Uncle Sam's part of your wealth. When you walk out for the final time, the tax problem walks in, and your good Uncle doesn't want the brick or steel or inventory or bonds that you have amassed – he wants the cash!

An accounting friend who does estate tax returns calls this "counting the dead." How many of your hard earned dollars will be paid to the United States Treasury simply because you happened not to wake up one morning?

Simply put, you have Good Assets (GA). These are defined as: when 100% of the asset goes to your heirs at death. Under today's rules, the maximum amount of Good Assets you are allowed is $5 million. The number may change in the next few years, but for now, it is $5 million. Next, you have Bad Assets (BA). Here, only about 50% of the asset will go to your heirs due to estate and inheritance tax. Sadly, there is no limit to how many of these assets you may have. And worst, you may have Really Bad Assets (RBA). In a worst case scenario, only 20 to 25% of the assets will go to your heirs due to estate, inheritance, and income taxes. Again, there is no limit to how many of these assets you may own.

The most motivating question I have ever devised to kick off a conversation about estate planning is: "'Realizing now that up to 80% of your wealth is going to be taxed away, should we do something about it?" It's amazing how many times the answer is a resounding yes!

XI. SETTLING THE ESTATE

One of the least understood – and consequently most often overlooked – aspects of the estate plan is settlement. For all the reasons expressed earlier, I favor the use of a team of advisors to walk you (or your executor) through the estate settlement process. The larger the estate, the more you need this team. Ideally, this team has already been assembled and working on your behalf prior to death so that the key elements of a smooth settlement are in place.

For estates of significant size, one of the most important elements is liquidity. Here, I define liquidity as the cash on hand to do all the things that need to be done by an executor and/or Trustee when it is required of them. This sounds simple, and it can be, but only when properly planned for ahead of time.

The following are just some of the liquidity issues you may face. Estate taxes are due to the Treasury nine months from the date of death; most states offer inheritance tax discounts to the estate if the taxes are paid within 60 days of death; attorneys and accountants need to be paid as the settlement progresses; funeral home and final expenses need to be paid within 30 days (sometimes sooner); mortgages and payrolls need to be paid at least monthly, and so on.

Without proper liquidity planning, your executor or your Trustee could be forced into a fire sale of your assets. The best of your assets could go for the least amount. Think about the situation where a business competitor of yours finds out your business is in distress because its principal is no longer living. Might they swoop in for "a deal," trying to buy up your best assets for the least amount? Or lure away your best employees while the enterprise is at a weak point? Or what about the family beach house or cabin? Would you want your family to be forced to liquidate a prized family property simply to meet some arbitrary, but ultimately mandatory, timeline from the IRS?

Not all estates are comprised of high profile assets like business interests or beach houses, but what about the simple act of settling even the most humble of estates? The cost to settle the first estate could have serious effects on the survivor's wellbeing. We have all seen the case where the death of a spouse causes a severe curtailing of lifestyle for the survivor if significant Social Security and pension benefits are lost.

Any good estate plan takes into account these contingencies. Your CPA can figure the tax your estate owes down to the penny once he/she is done with the calculations, but a really thorough estate plan should anticipate the final count well ahead of time. It should plan to reduce the casualties where possible and bring in reserves where needed. This reserve unit is "liquidity." Liquidity means cash; money to pay the bills, the taxes, and all the other unforeseen expenses of settling and disbursing an estate.

The most common, and often the best, form of liquidity is life insurance proceeds. Recall that the government wants the juiciest assets as payment, usually cash and marketable securities. But if we are trying to avoid the sell-at-all-costs scenario, then what we really need at death is cash, and sometimes, we need lots of it.

One of my insurance colleagues puts it this way: If paying taxes is like throwing money down a rat hole, why not throw the worst kind of rat poison: life insurance? By this, he means, no one likes buying life insurance. No one likes collecting on it either – it means they died! So, of all the financial things you own that you would most associate with the ugly act of paying taxes, why not use the financial instrument you likely despise most? Use life insurance as the cash to pay off Uncle Sam so that you can keep all your "important" assets intact.

Here's a simple example for our analytical friends: let's assume you fail to wake up one morning. After a few trips to the CPA, your executor is presented with a tax bill of $250,000 to settle your estate.

If there are four stacks of money on the table between your executor and the Treasury agent sent to collect the tax on your estate, keeping in my mind that this is *your* money, which stack do you want you executor to hand over to the agent?

1) $250,000 cash

2) The sale of a $350,000 taxable asset which becomes $250,000 after 30% income tax is paid

3) $500,000, the total out-of-pocket cost for your estate if it has to borrow $250,000 at 8%

4) $62,500, the amount you would have to invest today at 8% after-tax for 20 years to reach $250,000 by the time you die

If this were a multiple choice quiz, you would likely choose #4 since this amount is the lowest. Unfortunately, it is highly unlikely that you would have the foresight to put away that much money 20 years in advance to pay off Uncle Sam. For most people, because they fail to plan, the practical answer turns out to be #1. This is likely not very appealing to you.

I suspect you would rather choose: #5) None of the above.

If so, then the "right" answer might be life insurance. Had I given an option #5, it might look very close to this.

5) $7,500 per year until you die, all of which will be refunded to your heirs *after* the $250,000 tax bill is paid.

Does this sound more palatable? I bet it does. But, let's be blunt. You would *never* buy this policy if someone met you in the street and said: "Hey, Dan, you need to buy this $250,000 life insurance policy. It will only cost $7,500 per year. Doesn't that sound great?!" When put so crudely and starkly, no one would make the decision to implement that kind of insurance.

What I hope you can learn from this is to get over the idea of avoiding buying life insurance because of what it is. Buy it for what is *does*, don't buy the insurance because it is a good investment; it is most certainly not a good investment. Buy it because it serves as tremendous leverage on the cash and assets that you do not wish to liquidate or give to the IRS.

Put another way, if you already have many logs on the fire, and many logs in reserve, why continue to chop down more trees? Why not start planting some trees for the next generation? Specifically, if you plant some of those trees in an Irrevocable Life Insurance Trust (ILIT), you can watch them grow very favorably. When life insurance is deployed inside a properly constructed and executed ILIT, the proceeds are income and estate free. These are the saplings for future generations to harvest.

An orderly transfer of your funds to provide liquidity, often through the artful use of life insurance, may be far more important to overall wealth accumulation and transfer than earning an extra percent or two on your capital now. The relatively small amount of capital that you may move from accumulation mode to liquidity mode will be used far more effectively as a protection against death taxes than as an additional log on the fire.

XII. CHARITY

When we have our client discussions about estate planning, we frequently get to the topic of charitable giving. There are many worthy organizations and nearly everyone has been touched by at least one. In fact, when asked, folks often easily rattle off the names of two to four charities that have been important to them.

When it comes to the discussion of how to avoid or reduce income and estate taxes at death, I always love asking this question. I know *exactly* how everyone will answer. The question is this: how much of Uncle Sam's money do you want to spend to support your favorite charity?

In case you haven't instantly figured out the answer, it is: all of it! Makes perfect sense to me. If you could direct all the money that Uncle Sam is trying to take from you to your favorite charities, why wouldn't you? You know it would be going down some public toilet somewhere in a Washington D.C. bureaucracy if you let it go to the IRS. So why not direct it specifically to the groups and organizations you know will use it wisely?

This is exactly the way to think about charitable donations at death. You already know this intuitively, but it has to be said. You do not really own 100% of everything you think you own. Some of everything you "own" is really partially owned by society because of a social lien called a "tax." When you redeem some of your IRA and you get a bill from the IRS, the lien is called "income tax." When you sell a stock for a profit, the lien is called a "capital gains tax." And when you die, the lien is called "estate and inheritance" tax.

In almost all cases, you cannot relieve yourself of the obligation – except, in the case of charitable giving. Because of the "social lien" against most of your assets, you must settle up with the society at large when you die. You can do this by paying your taxes to the government or you can satisfy your lien by giving a roughly equivalent value of assets to charity. While the lien must be satisfied, the choice of paying up in the form of taxes is up to you. This may sound strange, but it is true: all estate and inheritance taxes are ultimately voluntary.

They are voluntary because, you *choose* to pay them. In the simplest example, I die. If I die with no estate planning in place, the lien is paid in the form of taxes because the "default" option (as written by the government) is to pay taxes. But if my will says "All assets go to Charity ABC and Charity XYZ", then I may be able to change the circumstances. Assuming Charities ABC and XYZ are, in fact, legitimate charities under the IRS code, I pay $0 in tax of any kind. None. Zip. Zilch. Goose Egg. My lien is satisfied by directing a portion of my assets to charity instead of to Uncle Sam.

Realize that you must take control and affirm your desire to pay your "social capital" directly to charity rather than to the IRS. Of course, if I wish to leave some of my assets to my heirs, I am (and they are) subject to inheritance and estate tax. But again, the tax is voluntary. I do not have to pay them so long as I leave the appropriate amount of assets to the right entities. If, however, I really want to leave *all* my assets to my family, then that is my prerogative. The law now says I have to pay taxes. Once the taxes are incurred, paying them is most definitely *not* voluntary!

In general, there are four kinds of giving:

1) Obligatory – United Way through work as an example. Your employer says or implies that you *must* do this.

2) Social or fun – Supporting the local football team candy fundraiser or charity golf outing

3) Passionate – Helping out the organization or activity that you love – usually with time, talent, and treasure

4) Strategic and transformative – The big kahuna of gifting. These are the gifts that make an institution or a campaign so successful that

the organization is catapulted forward into a new level of service and performance.

There are many strategies for charitable giving and there are many worthy causes. The important thing to do is find your passion. If you have the commitment and the passion, then the size of the gift is irrelevant. A good team of estate planners can tailor the best options for you to consider – whether large or small gifts.

My favorite example is that of an elderly woman who thought she could not make a difference in either of the lives of her grandchildren or her favorite charity because she "only had a $100,000 to give." Presumably, she had seen many larger gifts being given and she figured that the $50,000 she could leave her grandkids and the $50,000 she could leave the charity would not be the transformative gifts she had hoped to make.

As it turned out, she was fixating on the idea that only a six-figure gift could make a difference. She agonized over the final disposition of the assets – should it go to her grandchildren or her charity? What would the grandkids think if it went to charity? What would the board of the charity think of their longtime colleague if she gave all the money to the grandkids and none of the money to the charity? Quite a dilemma.

Well, the answer was simple: give a $100,000 gift to *both* the charity and the grandkids. There, that's easy! What? Doesn't sound right to you? Let me explain.

The solution is a Charitable Lead Trust. The details are beyond us here, but suffice to say, the charity got the full $100,000 bequest. It came with a few strings attached however. The charity was allowed to take the income off the $100,000 principal at 5% per year for 20 years. Do the math and you will see that $5,000 a year for 20 years yields $100,000 to the charity. At the end of 20 years, the principal, plus any additional growth, gets returned to the grandchildren. Everyone wins.

This is the kind of power a good estate team can offer you in creative planning.

XIII. STRATEGIES

If you have gotten this far without jumping chapters, I applaud your perseverance. You will be well rewarded from here on. This is where the interesting ideas and experiences of others come out. Beware, there will be more details and terminology, but you should find some very helpful ideas along the way.

Most successful people reach a point when they no longer benefit personally from their efforts. They have accumulated sufficient wealth such that earnings from a job, a business, or investment are more than they will ever need. Quite frankly, they have built so much capital that they could not use it all up no matter how long they live. If you have done an appropriate job in executing your retirement plan, you too will eventually come to the realization that you will not use all the money you have amassed in your lifetime.

The cruel irony is that the tax code penalizes the people who have made it to this point in their lives. Quite literally, because of estate taxes and liquidation costs, your beneficiaries could lose out on nearly 50% of your efforts, maybe more. What this means is that every additional dollar of capital you amass may be cut in half.

The "creative" – and fun – part of estate planning is trying to find a set of solutions to this question: would it make sense to borrow a tiny piece of your estate and set it aside to ensure that the entire estate passes on intact? In other words, can we pass on more assets to family and/or charity by removing some assets from the accumulation mode and putting it into a "wealth maximization" mode? The answer is often yes. Here are some examples that are reasonable for most people to consider.

1) *A-B Bypass Trust.* In your will, or RLT, you can designate that your estate be set aside in Trust until both you and your spouse are deceased. At all times, you and your spouse have access to the income and principal, but because of the way in which you own

the assets, both of your estates can pass estate tax-free, up to the maximum exemption amount, to your children.

2) *Charitable Remainder Trust (CRT)*. If you followed the Charitable Lead Trust example above, the CRT is just the opposite. You can leave money in trust, have it pay a guaranteed income to a family member for a specific number of years or over a family member's lifetime. At the end of the payout period, the remaining principal in the Trust can then be paid to a charity or group of charities.

A favorite aunt of mine did this very thing and it worked perfectly. She was a spinster, having lived with her sister all her life. Over time, the sister passed away and eventually, all that remained of her family was a younger brother. Because neither she nor her brother had children, there were no obvious heirs. Her plan was to leave her funds in a trust that would be used to take care of her brother should he outlive her. And he did. After his death several years later, her remaining funds went to two of her favorite charities.

3) *Wealth Replacement Trust (WRT)*. If you go back to the section on "Counting the Dead," you recall that I mentioned Good Assets, Bad Assets, and Really Bad Assets. Each asset you own can be categorized based on your estate plan to estimate how much estate tax you will pay. The WRT is an example of a different kind of asset, a Really Good Asset (RGA). I define an RGA as an asset that is worth 100% to 500% more when it goes to your heirs.

At first blush, this sounds absurd. How can you create an asset that is worth up to five times more when you die than when you are alive? Well, now that I have put it this way, can you guess what it is? It is life insurance. But, a special kind. Suffice to say, when you create a WRT, the idea is to leverage your annual gifts with life insurance so that the ultimate benefit reaches your family estate tax and income tax-free at a level one to five times higher than you have actually invested.

4) *Wealth Accumulation and Estate Preservation Investment Trust (WAEPIT)*. At some point in your financial life, you may get to that comfortable sense that you have more money than you will

ever need. While you may wish to continue controlling your investments, you will likely want to avoid income tax where possible while you are alive, and you most certainly will want to avoid death taxes when you die. This is the essence of a WAEPIT.

5) *A Charitable Gift Fund.* There are often times when you could use a large tax deduction but do not have an interest in "giving away" money to charity just to get the deduction. Alternatively, you may have a real fondness for several charities, but you may be afraid to commit too much of your charitable giving to one or the other's endowment. In either case, is there a way to do substantial charitable giving without giving up all the control?

Enter the Charitable Gift Fund. This particular type of instrument allows you to make unlimited gifts to a charitable fund. The contributions qualify as charitable gifts under normal charitable giving rules. However, instead of directly giving the assets to a single charity, the assets go into a "charitable foundation" which just happens to takes its direction from you (or an appointed successor). Of course, you cannot take back the money since it has been irrevocably given to a charity.

The major advantage to this approach is that the "charitable foundation" acts as a holding tank. The assets are invested, sheltered from income tax, and ultimately disbursed to the charities you designate so long as the charities are a recognized 501(c)3 entity. There are typically no annual minimum disbursements nor are there any maximums. You can select an investment strategy based on a menu of choices offered across the spectrum of conservative to growth oriented.

This approach is an excellent one when you have multiple organizations you like to support, when the number of gifts and the amount of gifts vary over time, or when you want to maintain control over the final distribution of the money, even well after you have passed away.

XIV. LONG TERM CARE

No section on estate planning will be complete without a discussion on long term health care issues. Cliché as it sounds, we could read several books on this subject and still not cover it all. It is a massive subject that is changing all the time. Nevertheless, there are some basic economic principles that you can master and use to your benefit regardless of the changing landscape.

First, let's be very upfront: by the time you learn all you need to know about long term care, you might already need it. So hiding behind the veil of "I need to learn more about it before I do something" is probably not a good approach. I advocate for making your best judgment at a time when all information is given, deciding on how to proceed, and then enacting a plan that gives you maximum flexibility to alter your course later if and when you think you should.

For purposes of our discussion on Long Term Care (LTC), I mean a situation where you or a loved one requires ongoing, specialized care for an injury or chronic medical condition. The required care is beyond your family's ability to provide it and the cost is substantial.

I have been fortunate in the sense that I have much firsthand knowledge of this exact situation. In my family, I have had six nonagenarians who have required one form or another of care – assisted living, nursing home care, critical care, etc. While I will not comment on the quality of care in various facilities, I will say that the more money you have to deal with this issue, the better your chances are of having quality care in a nice environment. As with most things, money talks when it comes to long term care.

Among the many unnerving aspects of LTC is the sense of uncertainty. When someone you love is in long term care, you can easily feel like you are being held hostage to the situation because you never know when the care will end, or what the ultimate cost will be. This is in addition to the truly draining emotional and psychological toll that any LTC situation takes on a family.

But there are ways to alleviate or eliminate the economic burden that a LTC situation can bring. In the chapter on insurance, I discussed several financial instruments that can be used in LTC planning. This is not an exhaustive list, but it is a good starting point for planning purposes. Again, I stress that familiarity with these terms is the starting point. A detailed financial plan with your estate planning team is crucial in making this planning efficient and effective.

XV. CONCLUSION

While the full scope of estate planning may appear to be overwhelming, I hope I have given you a framework by which you can examine the most important aspects of your estate plan. A well-crafted and implemented retirement plan with the requisite retirement income plan should adequately cover the questions of "what if I live/what if I live a long time?" The appropriate documents like a Power of Attorney or a Revocable Living Trust can help you negotiate the case of a temporary or permanent incapacity. Well-planned wills, trusts, and beneficiary designations can cover the eventuality of your demise. In the end, the success of your estate plan is measured by only one thing: how well it carried out your wishes.

Estate planning is an ongoing process. Tax laws change, new and improved trust arrangements may become available, and certainly the circumstances of your own life will change with time. At the very least, we ask our clients to review the fundamentals of their estate plan once a year. Absent any major legal or life changes, we undertake a more thorough review about every five years to make sure that the official documents like wills, trusts, and beneficiary designations are up to date and that they reflect your current wishes. You owe yourself the time to carefully consider how you will disburse your legacy; it is time well spent to reflect upon the good you have done and will do in your lifetime.

Chapter Seven

MISCELLANY

Business Planning, Horror Stories, Interesting Ideas,
and the Five Minute Primer

I. BUSINESS PLANNING

This book is clearly not long enough to include an extensive discussion on the economics of running a business. While many of our clients do in fact own a business, this is not the forum in which to discuss business matters. The subject is just too expansive. Throughout this book, I have discussed specific issues that may have an impact on a business interest, but now I would like to discuss specific elements of business ownership that might be used to your advantage in personal financial planning. For example, a personal IRA is a fine tool, but it is no match for a one-man 401K plan or a SEP-IRA account that can only be established by a business owner. Frankly, business owners have certain financial options at their disposal that regular employees just don't have. Here are a few ideas that merit consideration:

A. Retirement Plans

One of the few remaining perks of owning a business is the phenomenal leverage the owner can gain from using a tax-qualified retirement plan. While the ordinary employee can usually set aside at most only about $22,000 per year toward his/her own retirement, a business owner has the opportunity to put away as much as $150,000 annually – tax deductible and tax deferred until withdrawal.

Most people are aware of the standard 401K and the 403B plans, or tax sheltered annuity plans. In many circumstances, these are quite adequate, but a well-coached business owner using his tax and investment advisors' counsel will find that there are several alternative plans that allow for substantial tax savings while funding a retirement plan. Obviously the details of your particular situation will determine which ones make the most sense. Nevertheless, there are a few remaining ways to get money out of your business on a tax favored basis. A well-crafted retirement plan, or even a layering of two different sorts of plans, allows you to maximize both current tax savings as well as future retirement income.

B. Key Man Coverage

Assuming that your business is the basis for your livelihood, protecting that asset should be of the utmost importance. Depending on the size and scope of your business interest, the risks associated with that asset will be varied.

One question to ask yourself is: Other than you, is there someone so highly skilled or valuable that their loss would severely jeopardize your profitability? Or, you could think of the issue in terms of this question: Who, besides you, is responsible for the profits of this business?

Identifying one or two people in your firm that are integral to its success is probably not a new idea. Likely, you have been taking care of these people all along with bonuses, time off, etc. That kind of care and attention is important, but it is different from the idea I wish to present.

How much pain (financial or otherwise) will you feel if this person is unable to perform either due to untimely illness, death or departure? What is the financial impact of such a loss? Is there a way to create an offsetting influx of cash to sustain the business while you try to recover? In short, how can you protect against the financial loss of such an event? Key Man insurance is generally the answer.

Key Man insurance can be structured to provide cash to the business when you need it most, at the point of a major economic loss due to death, disability, or unforeseen departure. Your financial planner and CPA should assist you with evaluating this prospect and the products to address this risk. Often, an insurance specialist will be consulted to assist in designing more complex programs.

C. Business Continuation

This idea of financial "continuity" can be extended. What if the Key Man happens to be you? Clearly, if you voluntarily walk out the front door, there is time to plan and craft a reasonable transition. But what about the involuntary situation?

This area of thought is generally known as Business Continuation Planning. How will the business survive after your departure – either by death, incapacitation, or retirement – and how will you and your family be able to continue the benefits of business ownership?

Generally speaking, the objectives of Business Continuation Planning are:

1) Continue income to the owners (you and your family) after retirement or

   pre-mature death

2) Treat the children fairly – assuming one or more of your children want a stake in the business, how will you handle the distribution of wealth associated with the business? Specifically, how do you compensate the child(ren) who do *not* want to participate in the business?

3) Retain control until you are ready to pass the torch.

4) Minimize taxes – all forms, income, estate and gift.

5) Diversify – Provide additional security by diversifying wealth away from the business.

6) Remain flexible – leave options open for you and for future generations.

Please recognize that I have arbitrarily chosen the order of the objectives. In fact, I have likely left out at least one important issue that may have popped into your head. The point is that there are many issues to consider when you ponder the future of your business and the specter of it being run by another party. Regardless of your concerns, there are plenty of planning options available and a well-rounded team of your accountant, attorney, and financial planner can address the vast majority of these issues.

D. Children as Successors

One of the most difficult decisions I have seen business owner clients wrestle with is the idea of handing the reins over to a child. Sometimes, it is an uncertainty in the ability of the child to actually run the business. Other times, the child is uncomfortable with having a parent looking over his/her shoulder.

In my mind, this is as much a matter of business judgment as it is of familial harmony. Will the family business "survive" being run by a child while the parent looks on and perhaps a jealous sibling or two lurks in the shadows? Certainly, most situations do not involve this much intrigue, but there is a reason that most family businesses never make it past the second generation; a third generation-run family business is very rare indeed.

Realizing that your business can absorb the small mistakes you may make, it is also true that big mistakes may absorb the whole enterprise. This is a very serious question: Would your children be able to run the business without you? Can you be certain that your children will be able to run this business well enough to guarantee you don't have to work anymore?

If the answer is yes, then I have another, less painful, but more pointed question. Why are you still working?!

If the answer is honestly no, then you still have some work to do. What actions can you take now to address the long term well-being of your company, your spouse, and your family?

E. Business Disability Insurance

In the insurance section, we discussed that disability insurance protects the vital asset of future income. There are several kinds of disability insurance to consider in this situation: personal coverage, partner coverage, and key man coverage.

When you, the business owner, take a vacation, who pays the bills? Well, of course, you do. The business keeps running while you are away, revenue continues to flow, and you pay the bills when you get back. But what if your vacation is one year and unplanned? Meaning, what if you are disabled for a year and are unable to perform? Can the business keep paying you? This is where personal disability coverage fits.

What if the same "unfortunate absence" were to befall your business partner? Would you enjoy doing *all* the work and still *sharing* the profits? I suspect not. And I suspect your partner would not want you to either. Again, disability insurance – this time in the form of partner coverage – covers both of you. It protects both of your incomes and the integrity of your business relationship.

As I referenced earlier, you should also consider key man disability insurance to protect against the temporary loss of an employee vital to your success. Typically, a top salesman, a major figure in your operations, or a key account liaison is a candidate for this coverage if their loss would have a significant impact on your top line.

F. Buy/Sell Agreements

The final part of this discussion has to do with transfer of ownership when a death, permanent disability, or retirement occurs. If you die owning a business interest, what guarantee do you have that someone will buy that interest at a fair price? Frankly, without a buy/sell agreement, you have no guarantee. Will you want your family to be a creditor of the business? Especially after it has just lost its major driving force? Most people want to know that their family is taken care of regardless of what shape the business is in before and after your departure.

A buy/sell agreement is a legal contract that sets a price (or a formula for calculating the price) for your business interest. It defines a buyer and it sets the terms for the sale. The contract is enacted *before* the triggering event, presumably while all parties are on equal footing and under no duress.

Just as in any business setting, you do not want to work from a position of weakness. If your family loses you and has none of your future income to depend on, it will be very difficult for them to stand firmly and bargain a reasonable price for your share of the business. Thus, it is vital that the agreements be put in place when all parties are on equal footing.

Moreover, such an arrangement doesn't just protect you in the event of your death, disability, or retirement, it also protects you in the opposite situation. Assume *you* are the survivor. In the case of an untimely death of a business partner, who will your new partners be? How will you buy out their interest? Do you want to? Do you want to go into business with your partner's spouse? Probably not.

The fundamental economic question is: Where will you or your partner find the money to buy out the other? Would you prefer to liquidate company assets at distressed prices, or would you prefer to have a properly funded game plan in place? Simply put, proper buy/sell planning is the key to a smooth and economically satisfying transition of business interests.

G. Retirement Planning

While retirement planning in general is discussed in another chapter, there are a number of unique challenges presented for a business owner.

The average American retiree leaves a job from an employer. He/she takes a pension perhaps, probably a 401K or a 403B, maybe even a severance package. There may be medical benefits associated with the retirement plan. Do companies still give gold watches? In any event, the employee retires with something in hand, and that something has been given or provided by the employer.

If *you* are the employer, then anything you walk out the door with has had to be planned by you – or by your advisory team. Any long range benefit, like a profit sharing plan, 401K plan, extended medical benefits plan, or a deferred compensation plan, derives from your own foresight about retirement. Planning is crucial, and as always, the earlier you start, the better.

There are as many ways to accomplish this as there are different types of businesses. No one approach is right for everyone, but there are some common traits to good retirement plans that seem to work in many situations.

In broad terms, you need to have an exit strategy. How will you leave the business on the most favorable terms? Such a plan revolves around several crucial issues:

1) When will you exit and on what basis? Will you retire all at once, never to return, or part time over several years, or will you agree to stay on full time through a transition period where you go from employer/owner to employee?

2) Will you sell the business outright? Or will there be a phased-in buyer that requires your attention for some number of years?

3) Will there be a buyer from within like a family member or an important associate?

4) What will be your connection to the business be like over time? Will you want to stay connected, or will you simply walk away one day?

There are, of course, other issues. But generally speaking, the remainder will fall out in the wash after these basic questions are answered in detail. In any case, the role of your retirement advisor is to assist you in managing cash flow and investment considerations. While considerably different from other types of investments, a serious stake in a privately held business can be managed in the same way that any other retiree would manage his affairs. Creating an income plan that addresses both short and long term needs while balancing the risks of an investment portfolio is still the best approach to ensure you enjoy your remaining time on this earth.

In summary, please realize that while you may be retiring from life's work, you are retiring to something else. That something is becoming the CEO of your own retirement and estate planning business. Can you do this yourself? Should you? Or will you hire an expert manager to help? I want you to know, I might be applying for that job.

II. DECISION MAKING AND TAKING ACTION

One of my early mentors used to remind me of this adage: "Even if you are on the right track, if you are not moving in the *right* direction, at the *right* speed, when the train comes, you still get run over."

Knowing what needs to be done is not enough. Knowing that you need to do the right thing and knowing what the right thing *is*, is not enough either. You must know all these things *and* have the fortitude to do something about it.

One of the more difficult aspects of financial planning is the actual implementation of a plan (not necessarily the paperwork and bureaucracy, although this can be somewhat cumbersome). Given the final set of options, how do you make the final decision to go ahead with the one and best option you see?

For some folks this is easy. In fact, there are times when we jump right to the implementation because some folks don't want the diagnosis and the differential, they just want the prescription. Their attitude is: "Tell me what I need to do, show me how to do it, and make me do it now." There are not a lot of this kind of people, but if you are one of them, I suspect you already know that.

Hypothetically, if your doctor handed you a prescription today, would you fill it? Right away? I bet you would. But it doesn't always work that easily in a financial planning context. More likely than not, you are one of those people who needs time to consider your options and discuss them with your spouse, children, or some other trusted person in your circle. The vast majority of people fit this category.

Because of the gravity of the decisions you may feel you are making – after all, this is your life's economic work we are talking about – many people cannot always articulate what they are thinking or what is bothering them about making certain decisions.

Chances are you will not be in a position to make a decision on truly important matters on the very day that you are presented with the options. But what can often be difficult is articulating your feelings. If you are not comfortable with the advisor or not interested in the recommendation or presented solution, it would seem obvious to say so. But that is not always easy for people to do. In fact, it is not always easy to even understand why you might be uncomfortable.

Making a final decision can be difficult. When we look back on why some people are financially successful and others are not, it can often be traced back to the simple difference between those who could make a decision and those who could not. The successful are able to move forward, even when they are not entirely positive of the outcome, while those who are indecisive, never get around to taking any action.

If advisor and advisee are to have a productive and enjoyable relationship they each have to learn how to get around this potential hang up. First, let us realize that you will never have all the information you need to make a decision when it comes to financial matters. There are simply too many variables. Even if you did have *all* the information, then it would be a foregone conclusion, not a decision. Decision making by its very nature means filling in some of the blanks with educated guesses and well founded faith.

The good news is that this is a collaborative effort. This is where a great financial advisor and partner steps in to take the lead. Remember that it is precisely at these difficult times where a good advisor will be with you. While you may feel like you are in a very new and uncertain situation, it will likely be a very familiar one to the advisor. You will have to trust the advisor to be a good coach, teacher, and counselor. We will let you know what you need to know to make good decisions.

Procrastination usually comes about when people have a dilemma or disagreement, or some type of tension or stress. Sometimes, we know what the dilemmas or disagreements are; sometimes we can't quite put our finger on it. When I sense folks might be at an impasse, I offer up a straightforward question: "I am wondering why this decision seems so difficult right now. Sometimes people perceive a dilemma or they don't know how to proceed – is there anything like that going on with you right now?"

The simple act of hearing this question and then trying to verbalize an answer can break the logjam of indecisiveness. We both know that you may be uncomfortable venturing into unfamiliar territory – most folks are. In the end though, your financial future is too important to leave to chance, and we certainly cannot afford to let your future go unplanned. Should we make this decision today, or should we leave it up to unpredictable circumstance tomorrow?

III. HORROR STORIES – Some not so great moments in financial planning

A. Lucent Technologies

My father had a fictitious "I told you so" banner which he enjoyed unfurling in front of the people who failed to follow his advice. As he was often correct on the things he felt passionately about, he got to do this quite frequently.

I am not a big fan of doing this myself, but there is one classic example of "I told you so" in our area that occurred during the technology bubble of the early 2000's. A big employer in our area, Lucent Technologies, was known for good paying jobs with a nice benefit package including a fine 401K. As many companies were doing at the time, Lucent offered its stock to employees within the 401K world, including after-tax investment.

In the tradition of "invest in what you know," many people reasoned that they understood the company from the inside-out, knew its market potential with new technology, and saw the boom in internet investments. How could they go wrong?

At first, they couldn't go wrong! Lucent prospered, buoyed by sales to all manner of firms trying to build out their internet capabilities. The stock price rose. More employees were hired to fill the growing demand for design and production. The price continued to rise. Quarterly performance figures from the 401K began to catch people's attention and more and more people began moving their money from diversified mutual funds investments into the stock fund.

New sales records continued at the company. Profits began to build and a "things are different this time" mentality took hold. Yes, there *used* to be a business cycle in business capital spending, but this time is different. "Businesses will always need to buy our ever growing, technologically rich products and services – surely this income will continue without end!"

Record amounts of money poured into the stock. Mutual funds, private investors, and most of all, employees dumped money into the ever higher-flying stock. The more expensive it got, the more people wanted it. The price went over 50, then 60. Just when you thought it couldn't go higher, it went to 70, then a death-defying $80 a share.

Within a very short period of time – just a few months in some cases – ordinary middle managers became millionaires. In many cases, *multi*-millionaires. They had more money than they ever dreamed of. So what did they do?

Mercifully, some got out. Some realized this bubble for what it was and ran for cover. They realized they had already won the game and didn't need to make any more money. They had reached their financial goal – they had enough money to retire on, and they got out. But most did not.

Now, nine years later, I still periodically run into people who hold the now merged Alcatel-Lucent stock and are secretly hoping that the stock will go back up again. The millions they once had are now worth only a fraction of that amount.

The lesson to be learned here is many-fold. First, putting all your eggs in one basket is bad for your financial health. Second, keep your eyes on the prize: if collecting enough money to retire comfortably is the goal, then stop running once you have nicely crossed the finish line. By failing to realize they had safely reached their goals, these unhappy investors began to chase a "new goal" of amassing as much as they could. Their failure to realize that the truly important goal had already been attained set them up for the disturbing outcome of neither amassing a lot of wealth, nor being able to retire. Sad, but true.

B. The Ticking Time Bomb Called IRA

No, I do not mean Irish Republican Army, I mean the good old Individual Retirement Account.

In every part of this work, you will find me to be positive about IRA's. But you will also come to realize that the topic is somewhat complex and requires a fair amount of diligence in managing. This story is in that spirit; it involves a well-meaning father who tried to do the right thing, but failed to communicate his intentions, and an unsuspecting daughter who tried to do things quickly and "easily."

A widowed father had only one daughter and he wanted to pass the vast bulk of his estate to her. While he was educated and very involved in his own financial affairs, he did not (or could not) get his daughter involved with understanding his situation nor her own.

His plan seemed reasonable. He had money in retirement plans and personal investment accounts. As the retirement plans were tax-deferred during his lifetime, he rightly figured that the money would last longer if he first spent the non-retirement money since it would be more tax-efficient than using the retirement money. He also knew his IRA could pass to his daughter tax-deferred under an inherited IRA. The daughter would have to make minimum annual withdrawals on the IRA, and subsequently, she would have to pay the small amount of income tax due on those withdrawals. And, he also knew that she could stretch those payments out over her 40+ year life expectancy.

By now, you can guess that what the father knew, the daughter quite clearly did not. Or if she did, she did not fully understand the importance of the situation. When the father died, he left the daughter slightly under $100,000 of non-retirement money which was entirely tax-free to her. So far, so good.

The father also left over $1.3M in his IRA for his daughter. Had she taken the lifetime distributions as intended, she would have had the benefit of over $9M assuming minimum distributions and normal investment growth. Instead, she got a $680,000 income tax bill.

How? Rather than take the money as an inherited IRA, she rolled it over into her own IRA. This seemed reasonable to her as she had heard many people do it without a problem. She had read about it several times in the newspaper and in magazines, and since that option was on the beneficiary form provided to her by the 19 year-old, college drop-out "investment representative" at her father's IRA company, she marked the spot without hesitation or thought.

There's an old joke in our business: How do you make a small fortune? Take a large fortune and pay tax on it.

That's how over $9M turned into less than a tenth of that much for the daughter. The moral here is to communicate. Parents must share their intentions and plans with their children. Financial advisors must communicate meaningful and important information at the appropriate time, and they must anticipate that consumers may not really know what they want. The daughter *thought* she wanted a rollover IRA, but what she really needed was an inherited IRA.

I would also say that anyone trying to inherit an estate of this magnitude should not be doing so without professional advice. Think about it: even if the daughter had to pay $90,000 to get this done properly – an enormous and outrageous sum, I know – she still would be better off by several million dollars over time.

C. Pitfalls for the Unsuspecting and Unaware

The tremendous tax leverage that can be gained by using IRA's and 401K's allows folks to accumulate large sums of money in these vehicles. For many, these are the largest accounts they amass in their financial lifetimes. When unwound properly, the money that is distributed from these accounts can last for years and the tax-favored status of the money can be continued even across several generations. However, one poorly informed (or worse, entirely uninformed) decision can wipe out all previous accumulated tax savings and future tax-favored treatment.

Consider the case of a high level executive from DuPont whose family I happened upon several years ago. Ten months before I met the family, "Tom" had just retired from his employer of 37 years and was in very good financial shape. He had plenty of money, mostly in his 401K plan, and most of those funds were held in DuPont stock.

You have already read of the pitfalls that come with this kind of concentrated wealth; the level of risk you incur when most of your wealth is held in a single position is high. However, the financial nightmare derives not from the concentration of investment risk, but from poor tax planning. What made the above situation odd was the fact that the deed was done and the incredible loss of tax benefit was entirely unknown to the family when I came onto the scene.

Tom was ready, willing, and able to take on the world in retirement. Unfortunately, his heart was not. He suffered a massive heart attack, and died shortly after his retirement dinner. His family was, of course, devastated.

Rather than take the normal time to grieve and gather its wits after such a loss, the family immediately dove into settling Tom's estate. Because he had died in August, the children figured that they could save some income tax and administrative cost on the estate by settled everything by December 31. Add into the mix an overzealous, inexperienced human resource advisor at the company, and the dye was cast.

The crucial error occurred in the handling of the DuPont stock. In the tax code, there is a little known (and even less seldom used) section that allows for extremely beneficial tax treatment of company stock owned inside a 401K plan. Had only one person known about this, the family could have saved over $310,000 in income tax.

The problem began when Tom refused to take his 401K account at retirement and turn it into an IRA. Likely, you know that upon retirement or separation of service from your employer, you are eligible to move your 401K money either into a similar plan at your new employer or into a personal IRA. By failing to do the latter, Tom lost out on a very important opportunity to remove a huge chunk of tax-deferred money from his retirement account. Had he done so, using the Net Unrealized Appreciation (NUA) rules, he would have been able to withdraw all the stock and pay income tax on only the cost basis.

Certain corporate 401K plans purchased company stock at one time with *after* tax money even though the stock was held in a retirement account. The odd rules of NUA allow one to withdraw all the stock from this plan based on the after tax purchase cost (or cost basis) rather than the actual value at withdrawal. By paying income tax on the cost basis, Tom would have been able to remove over $1,000,000 of stock from his 401K plan for about $8,000. Now, that's tax leverage!

Of course, he would still have been liable for the capital gains tax on a future sale of the stock. At the time, capital gains tax rates were still at 20%, so he would have been facing a tax bill of 20% of $1,000,000 less the $32,000 cost basis. So, around $195,000 of tax would have been deferred under this plan. But – and this is a big but – the odd circumstances of his early death would have resulted in the elimination of that huge tax bill altogether.

Recall that when you die owning a capital asset, like a house or a stock or a mutual fund, all pending capital gains on those assets are forgiven in a "step up in basis at death" provision of the tax code. The IRS gives you a break when you die, believe it or not. In Tom's case, the $195,000 of potential capital gains tax that would have been payable when he sold the stock was washed away the day he died. He could have passed the entire stock onto his wife income and estate tax-free. Instead, he handed her a $1,500,000 IRA which was going to be entirely income taxable over her lifetime.

The good news is that the family was still fine and the spouse lived perfectly well on the residue of Tom's estate. But what about the huge amount of wealth squandered by nonexistent planning and uninformed judgment? Uncle Sam was the only beneficiary in this sad story. And I suspect Tom's reputation within the family may have suffered too.

I wonder if sometime in the future, Tom's children or grandchildren will look back on that situation and wonder: I thought Dad (or Grandpa) was so smart! I guess he wasn't the super smart guy we thought he was. Too bad.

IV. INTERESTING IDEAS

This section has no particular position in the book in that it does not follow progressively from other ideas. It is not meant to be part of an overall strategy that looks from a global prospective. Rather, it is meant to be a collection of interesting planning ideas that are specifically tailored to special situations. There is no particular order, so read the synopsis first. If the idea catches your attention, read on and you may find the idea helpful. If the situation doesn't catch your attention, feel free to jump ahead to the next one.

A. Remembering Grandparents

Try this exercise for fun. Take a sheet of paper and write across the top in four columns the full names of your four grandparents. Can you do that off the top of your head? Many people cannot. To make the exercise a bit more difficult, extend two lines down from each grandparent and try to write down the full name of each of your great-grandparents. I have yet to see someone be able to do that from memory.

What's the point? Well, do you think John D. Rockefeller's great-great-grandchildren remember his name? I bet they do! Why? Because his monetary legacy continues to them to this day.

One of the most special bonds in life is that between a grandparent and grandchild. One way that far-sighted grandparents seek to extend their relationships beyond their own mortality is by using a Remembrance Trust.

I use the term generically. An actual trust is not required to put this clever idea into action. The basic idea is a gift that keeps giving. While living, or at death, a grandparent can put money aside into an account that specifically pays a specific amount to the grandchild on his/her birthday. This can continue for the entire life of the grandchild, even though Grandma and Grandpa may be long passed.

This money may start out as a small annual amount when the child is young and then increase as needs (and wants) grow. Money can go toward education expenses in young adulthood. As the grandchild has children of his own, funds can go toward first homes, business start-ups, and any of the great challenges life offers.

I can't guarantee it, but I bet a grandchild who is the recipient of such a loving gift will certainly be able to write down *your* full name when they take the Name-Your-Grandparents test.

B. Multi-Generational IRA's

If you are fortunate enough to reach that all-too-strange age of 70 ½ years (thank you Internal Revenue Service for this odd choice of ages), you are faced with an annual decision of how much to withdraw from your IRAs to comply with the *Required Minimum Distribution (RMD)*. Obviously, your primary income needs come first and you should withdraw as much money as you need. But many folks are in the fortunate position of not needing the IRA money. The mandatory withdrawals are a nuisance since they trigger income tax on money that otherwise would not be taxed. Is there any good that can come from this? Enter the Multi-Generational IRA.

There are three twists on this theme, all of which serve different purposes. In each case, I am assuming that you are over age 70 ½ and that you are subject to the Required Minimum Distribution (RMD) rules that apply to all retirement accounts once you reach this age.

The first idea is very basic. Under the current RMD rules, you are required to take an annual withdrawal that increases each year as a percentage of the total in your retirement plan. For example, in the first year, the percentage withdrawal is less than 4% of the total; by the time you reach age 80, the amount is up to about 6%. At age 85, it's about 8%.

The upshot of this progression of ever higher percentage withdrawals often leads to a higher income tax bracket in older years. As the amount of taxable income from your retirement accounts steadily increases, you are eventually pushed, involuntarily, into a higher tax bracket. The solution is to simply "override" the effect of the RMD "push" by "annuitizing" your retirement money at age 70 ½. This, in effect, creates a lifetime payout stream that is steady over time (in amount of income *and* in amount of income tax), rather than the ever accelerating stream that can eventually push you into the next tax bracket (see the Income and Tax Trap chart).

A variation on this idea is based on another idea that most retirees can attest to: from the viewpoint of your own mortality, which set of ten years will be your best? The next ten years or your last ten years?

I have yet to hear someone say, "my last ten years." If this is so, then having more money to spend in the early part of your retirement seems to make a lot of sense. But recall that the RMD rules work in exactly the opposite fashion. They are designed to pay out less in the beginning stages and more as you age.

Enter the "joint payment" system. Similar to the "joint and survivor" option offered by most pension plans, this approach allows you to take a higher annual withdrawal in the early years without fear of bankrupting the account in later years. And just in case, we can add in a feature that pays a refund of the principal to your heirs in case you or your spouse die prematurely.

Income and Tax Trap at age 70 ½

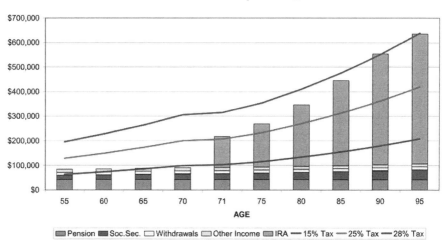

Pension · Soc.Sec. · Withdrawals · Other Income · IRA — 15% Tax — 25% Tax — 28% Tax

The third approach is to create a Roth IRA. Any holder of an IRA may convert a portion or all of a Traditional IRA into a Roth IRA. While this is a taxable event, the long term benefits can be astounding. The tax-free nature of a Roth over a long period of time can offer enormous leverage in creating family wealth.

First, we should recognize that such a conversion, because it is a taxable event, rarely imparts any value to the account holder. If you are going to use funds from your IRA during your lifetime, it would make sense that creating a Roth IRA is silly. Why pay income tax today on money you do not need until later? Only Uncle Sam seems to win in that case.

Where the value arises is in the inherited Roth IRA – a Roth IRA that passes on its tax-free status to your heirs. Assume you are age 65 with $100,000 in a Traditional IRA. If you were to convert this into a Roth IRA, you would pay about $28,000 in income tax. Painful, perhaps.

But the long term benefits can be astounding. Assume your Roth IRA investments grow at 12% annually. At your death, assuming your 35-year old daughter were the beneficiary at your death, and she lived to life expectancy, she would receive a total value of about $7.4M of tax-free benefit over her lifetime. If you named your four year old granddaughter as beneficiary, she would receive about $102.5M over her lifetime. Now that's power!

C. Millionaire IRA Planning

Because of the unique double taxation that IRA's and all other retirement plans are subject to at death, planning is vitally important for those who have an estate over $5,000,000. When planned improperly (or not planned at all), a person who dies owning a substantial IRA as part of a large estate will face both income tax (at roughly 35 cents on the dollar) and estate tax (starting at 45 cents on the dollar). This double whammy effect can cause 70-80% of the IRA assets to disappear on the same horrible day of your death. It will literally be the most expensive day of your life.

There are several options to prevent this circumstance – the tax part; unfortunately, not the dying part. An obvious solution is to provide your spouse with the ability to do a spousal rollover to preserve the income tax status on the money. Estate tax rules provide for an unlimited exemption for spouses in the case of a rollover, so we can eliminate (or at least significantly postpone) the estate tax issue in the same transaction.

However, a slightly different approach may yield better results. If we consider multiple generations of wealth, a Roth IRA conversion may be the better choice. This strategy can be tricky if the IRA holder is nearing death but can be worth pursuing. The value is in the tax rate discrepancy between federal income taxes and federal estate taxes. Because of the income tax credit that can be claimed against the estate tax (notice that 35% maximum income tax rate is better than 45% estate tax rate), we can simultaneously reduce the estate tax and create a "tax-free for life" IRA for your family. Assuming generation skipping tax is not an issue (see a good estate attorney for a complete explanation of this vast topic), a Roth IRA distributed over the lives of your spouse and your children and grandchildren can increase your family wealth many times over.

If you are the later of the two spouses to pass away, a rollover is not feasible. However, we can still use an inherited IRA to pass the money to your heirs. This will not reduce the estate tax, but it will defer the income tax significantly. Rather than incurring the income tax at the maximum rate in the year of your death, we can spread out the tax over the lifetime of the beneficiaries. Further, the tax rate may be diminished if the heirs are in a lower income tax bracket than you and your spouse.

One small caution on this idea is that our friends in Congress are notorious for changing the rules on us. While we know the income tax rates today, we do not – and cannot – know them five, ten, or fifty years from now. If your grandchildren inherit your IRA, who knows what the income tax will be for them. But even with this uncertainty, good advice from a forward thinking financial planner should be able to mitigate this risk over time.

D. Net Unrealized Appreciation.

In limited circumstances, a large 401K plan may be funded with company stock. In a situation where the cost basis on this stock is relatively low compared to the current value, a distribution under the Net Unrealized Appreciation (NUA) rules would be advisable to consider. This little used rule can assist you in removing from your 401K plan a large asset which normally would be subject to ordinary income tax rates, and turn it into an asset that instead is taxed at long-term capital gains tax rates. Since the current tax rates significantly favor long term capital gains – 35% at a max for ordinary income versus 15% for capital gains – this seems appealing. It becomes even more appealing when you realize that capital assets receive a step up in basis at death. This allows for the potential that virtually all of the capital gain may be eliminated from tax at your death.

E. Using Trusts

In special situations where a trust should be used, a properly crafted IRA Inheritance Trust can serve to shelter the IRA from income tax in a similar way to the inherited IRA. Further, the Trust can restrict the use of funds from reckless spending by a spendthrift beneficiary. Even if your children are very responsible with money, they may enjoy the creditor protection that such a trust can offer them. Failed marriages and failed business deals cannot affect the financial security that your IRA Inheritance Trust could provide for your children and grandchildren.

For those folks who prefer to maximize the amount of wealth they can transfer to their heirs, we can implement a Family Dynasty Trust. To enhance the legacy to one's family, we can systematically draw down the IRA assets in a controlled fashion during one's lifetime such that we minimize income taxes along the way. We then take the proceeds and transfer them into a Family Dynasty trust that is outside the donor's estate.

If we use a special kind of life insurance arrangement as the funding vehicle, we accomplish several objectives. First, we significantly reduce the income tax and estate tax liabilities by drawing down assets during life, while funneling them out of the estate. At death, the remaining (but much smaller) IRA can still pass by one of the above methods, but the much larger life insurance proceeds "pop up" in the trust. As you now know from the segment on life insurance, these proceeds are both income tax-free (because it is life insurance) and estate tax-free (because the Trust owns the policy outside your estate).

As in any sophisticated financial planning, this is not something you should be trying at home without a safety net and a helmet. And certainly, you should not be attempting this without a qualified estate planning attorney. Put more clearly, do not buy Estate-Planning-In-A-Bottle and Do-It-Yourself-IRA-Brain-Surgery software off the internet and expect to be able to do this yourself. You may delude yourself into thinking that you have saved a few dollars, but your heirs most likely will pay the severe price of you having done this incorrectly. I guess you could take solace in the fact that the IRS will thank you posthumously.

F. Early Access to Retirement Money – "Look, Mom, no penalty!"

Even the most casual observer of financial information knows that retirement money is generally hands off until age 59 ½. Any money withdrawn from an IRA, 401K, and the like prior to that age incurs income tax and a 10% penalty. Unknown to most folks though are several ways in which one can remove money from a retirement plan without incurring the penalty.

In the case of a 401K plan, a participant who is "terminated" – either dismissed or forced into early retirement – generally has access to the money if the separation from service occurred after age 55. However, this option is only available on the 401K plan of the employer which initiated the separation. It does apply to former employers' plans or to any other type of retirement money like an IRA.

While the use of this age 55 option is rare, a more popular method is known as 72(t). Just as the 401K plan is identified by its appearance in the Internal Revenue Code under section 401, subsection K, the 72(t) rules are likewise named. These rules are best left to be applied by the experts at your IRA custodian or your plan administrator. The concept, however, is simple.

If you withdraw money from any retirement plan prior to age 59 ½, you can avoid the 10% penalty if you take withdrawals based on a serious of substantial and equal payments that last for at least five years, or until the time you reach age 59 ½, whichever is longer. It sounds difficult, but it is actually easy to follow. If you are 57 when you begin the payments, you must continue until five years from that point, or age 62. If you are 51 when the payments begin, you must continue until age 59 ½.

The more cumbersome part of the rule is the "substantial" part of "substantial and equal." Obviously, if you start taking $5,000 in year one, it is pretty obvious that you must take $5,000 in year two, and so on in order to satisfy the "equal" requirement. There is one minor exception to this rule which applies to annuities being liquidated. If you liquidate the same number of sub-account units in each period, you will be deemed to be in compliance, even if the final dollar amount received based on the liquidations may be different. But this is a rare circumstance.

More often than not, the dollar amount will be constant year-by-year or, in the case of an early pension, month-by-month. Where the difficulty arises is in the concept of "substantial." What constitutes a substantial withdrawal? The answer lies in the age of the participant, the amount of money in the account, and the life expectancy method applied. While the mathematics of this is well beyond the scope of this conversation, suffice to say, an expert in this area is required to assure that your early retirement withdrawals satisfy the exemption from the 10% penalty. Based on your situation, a creative solution is often available, but in many cases like this, a professional opinion is preferable before you act.

V. FIVE MINUTE PRIMER

In other sections of this book, I have tried to delineate the major facets of what I consider personal financial planning. In each section, the goal has been to first outline the significant financial issues associated with each phase then to discuss the strategies, and in some cases, the financial instruments best suited to address those issues.

In this section, my goal is to offer a synopsis of these sections in a format that can act as a useable outline to track your financial progress. Rather than delve into the specifics of each financial stage of life, this section is meant to be a quick read. It is presented mostly in a series of questions and follows a natural progression beginning at the Accumulation Phase, continuing right through the Distribution Phase to legacy and estate planning (see the Five Steps of Financial Maturity). If you have good solid answers to these questions, then you have successfully conquered the particular stage and you are ready to move on. If not, then I suggest you begin your discussions with a financial planner on the particular topics that most interest you.

A. Retirement

Have you adequately covered the liability of your retirement? Based on some reasonable assumptions, we can calculate the amount of money you need to be saving on a monthly basis between now and the time you want to retire. The simple question is: does your current monthly budget include the savings necessary to fund your retirement? In the long run, are you going to outlive you money or will it outlive you?

If you are saving enough (although few people are), do you have an overall strategy for tripling your income over your retirement years? With the ravages of inflation over a projected 20 or 30 year retirement, can you provide an income you cannot outlive? Do you need to establish or update such a plan? If so, you need to begin discussing your thoughts and wishes with a competent financial planner.

Assuming that you have begun to amass assets for your retirement, were these investments chosen as part of an overall strategy? Do you have a comprehensive investment strategy or were these investments chosen piecemeal? Would you like to consider investment programs that are self-completing? Are you open to re-positioning some of these assets if they were better suited to your desires, or if you could reduce the tax liability on your portfolio?

Are you currently paying income tax on any income that you do not need to live on? Do you have long term investments that are unnecessarily exposed to current income tax liability? Assuming that you like your 401K plan and the tax-favored treatment of money within it, does it make sense to duplicate that environment in your personal investments but without all the red tape? Similarly, assuming that you understand the significant benefits that a pension plan offers, would you entertain the idea of creating your own private pension? Doesn't it make sense to take control over your own retirement plans by having an IRA rather than leaving behind old 401K's and the like at former employers?

B. Helping Yourself and Others

When you think about your family's future, will your children be able to give your grandchildren the same education you gave your own children? As one of my favorite clients once said, "I didn't come this far to leave my grandkids with student loans and dead end jobs. I think it is up to the three of us to get this education task done."

Inasmuch as demographers have identified your generation as the "sandwich generation," a group of folks who may simultaneously have to raise their own children and care for their elderly parents, do you anticipate the need to help your elder family members financially? Or instead, might there be an inheritance waiting for you? What plans do you have for either of these contingencies?

Consider the institutions that have made a difference in your life. Are there charitable institutions you would like to benefit? If we could use some of the wealth that would ordinarily go to the government in the form of estate and inheritance taxes, would you like to be able to channel those resources to charity? Will it be more meaningful to you to give those resources now while you are able to see the good they may produce?

For most people, over half of their lifetime medical expenses will come in the last five years of their lives. Realizing that chronic long term medical situations may be the biggest financial risk you face, what plan do you have for paying the medical bills if they should arise? Who will care for you? Who *should* care for you? Who will provide for your parents or elderly relatives if you cannot?

What would happen financially to your family or your business if tomorrow morning you breathe out and forget to breathe in again? This is a funny euphemism for: what happens to your loved ones if you die in your sleep tonight? What *should* happen? Should kids get educated, houses get paid off, businesses sold? What must happen for your family to be financially secure? Are your plans any different if that day comes ten years from now instead of tonight?

C. Estate Planning

If you have adequately answered the above questions and successfully navigated retirement, education planning, insurance, and investment planning, then you have one final hurdle. With success in the earlier stages of your financial life, you will have amassed a substantial amount of wealth along the way. How then do you want this money to intervene in the lives of your family and community while you are living? How about when you are no longer here to use it?

The financial fate of your family across the generations may hinge on these questions of inheritance and legacy. How will you pass on your wealth with a minimum of taxation? Some clients have said that the perfect inheritance is enough money that your heirs feel like they can do anything, but not so much money such that they feel they can do nothing. Give them the assets to accomplish great things; do not give them so much that they can sit around and do nothing.

What is most important to you about your own legacy? Is it about maximizing the inheritance to your family? Is it about conferring moral and ethical lessons about money? Is it about preserving a cherished family heirloom or vacation home? What should your financial legacy say about your personal legacy, if anything?

D. Working with a Planner

Beware, here comes the shameless plug for the financial planning industry of which I am a part. No matter where you are on this progression of thinking and planning, a dedicated financial planner who takes the time to get to know you well will make your planning and implementation much easier. Seasoned veterans have been down these roads before; they know the potholes, shortcuts, and oases. Use their wisdom and expertise to plot your own, unique course to financial success.

VI. REFERRALS

The highest compliment a planner can receive from a client is the referral of a friend or family member. It is the ultimate sign of trust. For a client to feel so comfortable and secure in recommending their family and friends reaffirms all that we, as client and advisor, have set out to do.

Whenever I approach a prospective client, I am really applying for a job as their personal advisor. Most prospective employers want references. There can be no better way for a person who is looking to hire an advisor to be confident in their choice than by having one of their most trusted friends make that introduction.

For the past several years, virtually all of our new clients have come to us through this introduction process. While I cannot guarantee that we can help every person who comes to see us, every person who comes to us by way of a personal referral will be treated like family. If you think enough of a friend or family member to take the time to introduce us to them, we owe you the courtesy to treat them like our friends and family.

Interestingly, I have had many occasions when existing clients have asked me who they could recommend. It is as if they feel a commitment to help our business grow. I certainly appreciate this vote of confidence and encouragement. To accommodate this request, I have accumulated a number of "ticklers" that often remind folks of people who they might suggest we talk with in the future:

1) Who do you have fun with? (Chances are if you and I get along well, then the people you enjoy spending time with will be people that I too will enjoy.)

2) If I threw you a cocktail party for your birthday, who would you want to invite?

3) Do you know people who really don't understand a particular financial planning issue, but want to?

4) Who would come to an educational program about financial matters?

5) What fundraising, charitable, or non-profit organizations do you deal with or participate in? Would such an organization need some assistance in dealing

with charitable giving or endowments?

6) Who are the most successful business people you know?

7) Who is expecting to retire in the next five years?

8) Who do you know who just retired?

These are just a few ideas to ponder. Naturally, I do not expect anyone to be sitting around thinking about who they can refer to our business. But when those rare opportunities arise, we recognize your kindness in making such an introduction is the most valuable form of advertising. It is truly priceless! Thank you.

APPENDIX MATERIAL

PERSONAL FINANCIAL GOALS

In order to discuss specific goals, please review this list and check off the items that are of most concern to you. Please think about your priorities and be prepared to discuss them.

SAVINGS/INVESTMENTS

_____ Establish an emergency fund
_____ Save and invest more systematically
_____ Increase investment returns
_____ Diversify my assets
_____ Use more appropriate vehicles
_____ Avoid/defer taxable income

FUTURE GOALS INCLUDE

_____ Making a large purchase (when?)
_____ Changing jobs/careers
_____ Funding a college education
_____ Changing marital status
_____ Insuring my family
_____ Insuring my income
_____ Retiring
_____ Generating investment income

RETIREMENT PLANNING

_____ Calculate how much I need to retire
_____ Review/supplement company plans
_____ Review/manage personal plans
_____ Pension maximization
_____ Evaluate a lump sum option
_____ Generate income from investments

EMPLOYER BENEFITS

_____ Review existing plans/options
_____ Coordinate with personal plans
_____ Evaluate level of coverage

LIFE/DISABILITY INSURANCE

_____ Review current coverage
_____ Evaluate level of coverage
_____ Review ownership/beneficiaries

INVESTMENT PROFILE

_____ Very conservative
_____ Moderately conservative
_____ Somewhat aggressive
_____ Very aggressive

CURRENT ADVISORS INCLUDE

_____ Accountant
_____ Attorney
_____ Stock broker/mutual fund advisor
_____ Insurance agent
_____ Financial planner

ESTATE PLANNING
_____ Review current plans
_____ Examine long term medical care
_____ Reduce federal estate taxes
_____ Structure a will or trust
_____ Coordinate beneficiaries, wills, trusts
_____ Increase charitable giving

OTHER ISSUES
_____
_____
_____
_____
_____
_____

Considerations for the Individual Trustee

An individual who consents to serve as a trustee is well advised to consider:

1) his general responsibilities as a fiduciary;

2) the terms of the trust;

3) the circumstances of the beneficiaries, the nature of the trust assets, and the investment policy to be followed for the trust;

4) the importance of acting prudently in all matters related to the administration of the trust; and

5) the critical support of good investment and legal advisors in assuring that the standard of prudence will be met.

Fiduciary and Trust Relationships

A fiduciary is someone who acquires any form of power or discretion over someone else's interests. A trust represents a particular type of fiduciary relationship, one that exists with respect to property. While the trustee holds legal title to trust property, and in that sense is the owner of that property, the trustee must use the property for the benefit of the trust beneficiaries. Given the breadth and scope of the power that flows from a fiduciary relationship, the subject of the fiduciary relationship, the beneficiary, can be vulnerable. To protect the beneficiary, the law imposes "fiduciary obligations" to control the exercise of fiduciary power by the trustee.

Trustees are Held Personally Liable

Illustrative of the seriousness with which the law seeks to control abuses of fiduciary discretion is the rigorous nature of the rules governing liability for breaches of trust. While an attitude that is respectful of one's fiduciary responsibilities is both appropriate and necessary, a good faith attitude alone will not necessarily assure the avoidance of fiduciary liability. The prudent trustee should never assume that honest and reasonable good faith conduct will be sufficient to avoid breaches of trust.

An action for breach of trust is brought against the trustee personally. If the trustee is found liable, the judgment is against the trustee in his individual capacity. Enforcement of the judgment is against the trustee's individual assets, not those of the trust. Under certain circumstances, a trustee may be entitled to indemnification from trust assets for liabilities of the trust properly incurred in the administration of the trust.

Categories of Trustee Liability

There are two broad categories of trustee liability:

1) liability of the trustee, as the legal owner of the trust property, to third parties who are not trust beneficiaries

2) liability to beneficiaries for breaches of trust.

Liability to Third Persons

Trustee liability to third persons (including governmental agencies) may arise from:

1) a trustee's contracts with third parties,

2) a trustee's torts committed against third parties, and

3) a trustee's status as a holder of title to trust

Liability to Beneficiaries

A trustee can be personally liable to trust beneficiaries for negligent or intentional breaches of duties, which cause injury to the trust. A breach of trust occurs when a trustee violates any fiduciary duty. To avoid a breach of trust, trustees must be familiar with each of the myriad of fiduciary duties.

Usually, when a trustee commits a breach of trust, he will be personally at fault. He may violate a fiduciary duty in bad faith. He may be negligent. But he also may be liable when he acts in good faith and takes what he believes to be a reasonable action. Examples of such would be:

1) A trustee potentially will be liable for a mistaken payment or distribution of trust property to someone who is believed to be a beneficiary but who is not actually entitled to a distribution.

2) A trustee will be liable if he takes an action, which is believed to be within the scope of his authority under the terms of the trust but which, in fact, exceeds that authority.

Accordingly, the prudent trustee who may be in doubt about to whom a trust distribution should be made (or any other fact) or about the scope of his authority to act (or any other matter of law) is well advised to seek legal counsel and apply for court instruction.

Other Miscellaneous Liabilities Reporting

Trustees may have reporting obligations with respect to voting rights or powers of disposition over more than a certain percentage of a class of registered securities, and may suffer criminal and civil liabilities for failure to register under federal and state securities laws as well as for insider trading violations.

Taxes and Tax Decisions

Trustees have obligations with respect to federal and state income, gift, estate or inheritance, and generation-skipping transfer (GST) taxes.

The opportunity is ever present for error by the fiduciary, which can result in civil penalties and criminal violation with serious financial consequences.

Misappropriation/Misuse of Trust Funds

A trustee who uses trust funds as if they were his own, intending to misappropriate them, commits the crime of embezzlement.

Trustee Duties

Duty to be generally prudent

A trustee has a duty to act reasonably and competently in all matters of trust administration. The standard of care is that which a person of ordinary prudence would exercise in dealing with his own property. If the trustee either possesses, or has represented that he possesses, greater skill than that of a person of ordinary prudence, liability will follow for losses resulting from a failure to use greater skill.

Duty to carry out the terms of the trust

A trustee has a duty to carry out the intentions of the settlor as determined by the terms of the trust. The extent of a trustee's duties and powers is determined by the trust instrument and applicable rules of law, not the trustee's interpretation of the instrument or the trustee's belief as to the applicable rules of law. Whenever in doubt, a trustee should seek an opinion of counsel or court instructions.

Duty of loyalty

The trustee's duty of loyalty, i.e., the duty to administer a trust solely in the beneficiaries' interests, is the most fundamental duty owed by the trustee to the beneficiaries. The proper discharge of this duty requires the trustee to act selflessly by putting the beneficiaries' interests before the trustee's personal interests. The duty of loyalty may be breached in numerous ways, one such example is:

A direct conflict of interest

The clearest breach of the duty of loyalty occurs in a case of self-dealing. One clear example of self-dealing is where a trustee buys property from or sells personal property to a trust. In such cases, the "no further inquiry" rule applies. Beneficiaries may apply to a court to have a self-dealing transaction set aside, regardless of the trustee's good faith. They also may elect to hold the trustee accountable for any profit made on the transaction; they may compel the trustee to restore property to a trust if it has been purchased from a trust; or they may compel a trustee to repurchase property sold by the trustee to the trust.

Duty to keep and render accounts

A trustee has a duty to provide clear and accurate accounts to the beneficiaries, showing in detail the nature and amount of the trust property. A trustee who fails to keep proper accounts will suffer the consequences. A trust may provide that the trustee is not required to formally account to a court. Such a provision may be effective to avoid a formal court accounting if it is not found to violate a statute. Provisions stating that a trustee does not have a duty to account to beneficiaries may be deemed to violate public policy.

Duty to provide information

A trustee is required to provide complete and accurate information concerning the nature and amount of trust property and to allow inspection of the trust property and accounts, vouchers, and other documents. A beneficiary may inspect legal opinions obtained by the trustee to guide him in the administration of the trust. On the other hand, opinions obtained by the trustee at his own expense for his own protection are privileged.

Duties to take and keep control of, preserve, separate and earmark trust assets

A trustee must promptly take possession and control of all trust assets, preserve them, and protect them from loss or damage. Assistance in safekeeping trust assets may be provided by brokers, bankers, and custodians retained by a trustee. A trustee is required to keep trust property separate from his own property, to keep the property of any particular trust separate from the property of other trusts, and to take title to trust property in the name of a trust.

Duty to make property productive

A trustee must use reasonable care and skill to make trust property productive in a manner consistent with the fiduciary duties of caution and impartiality. The duty of caution requires that investments be made with a view to the safety of capital and for a reasonable return. Safety of capital means real, as well as nominal, value. Thus, a trustee should invest to mitigate the risk of loss of purchasing power through inflation. Return refers to total return, including capital appreciation and gain as well as income. Capital growth may include growth in real value in addition to the preservation of purchasing power.

Duty to deal with multiple beneficiaries impartially

Whenever a trust has two or more beneficiaries, a trustee has a duty to deal with them impartially—a duty that raises difficulties with respect to investment issues. In trusts that separate beneficial interests into those entitled to receive income and those entitled to the remainder, balancing these interests may be difficult. With a traditional distinction between income and principal, which does not take into account the investment concept of total return, investing for maximum income may sacrifice growth. At the same time however, investing for maximum growth may jeopardize the income beneficiary's right to

income. In contrast, an investment strategy that focuses on total return may produce greater financial benefits over the long term than a strategy that focuses on the production of current income.

Duty of prudent investment

Formerly, a trustee's duty of care and prudence in managing trust investments was determined under the "prudent man rule." As applied by the courts, this rule tended to define permissible types and characteristics of trust investments, and judged investments on an asset-by-asset basis in isolation from their performance in the context of a portfolio.

In 1990, the American Law Institute promulgated the Restatement (Third) of Trusts, which replaced the prudent man standard with the prudent investor rule. Under the prudent investor rule, no investment assets or management techniques are imprudent per se. In addition, the prudent investor standard develops five principles outlined below:

1) Diversification is fundamental to risk management and generally is required of trustees.

2) Market risk is unavoidable in investing. Trustees have a duty to analyze and make conscious decisions about the levels of investment risk appropriate to the return requirements, risk tolerance, general purposes, specific terms, distribution requirements, and other circumstances of trusts that they administer.

3) Trustees must avoid unnecessary fees and transaction costs.

4) The duty of impartiality requires a balancing of the elements of total investment return between the production of current income and the protection of purchasing power.

5) Trustees may have a duty, as well as the authority, to delegate investment management responsibilities to others. The duty of prudent investment may require more knowledge and experience with investment matters than the trustees may possess, depending on the investment strategies to be used. Trustees may be required to obtain competent advice, guidance, and assistance in order to meet their investment responsibilities.

Prudence is required in the delegation process. While trustees are not required to personally perform all aspects of the investment function, they may not abdicate their responsibilities. At a minimum, they must define the trust's investment objectives, but they may do so with the benefit of professional investment advice. Trustees must make decisions about a trust's investment strategies and programs. This may consist of approving plans that are developed by advisors or agents.

If trustees decide to delegate responsibility, prudent care must be taken in selecting competent agents to whom duties will be delegated, in negotiating and establishing the terms of the delegation (including the agent's compensation and the duration and conditions of the delegation), and in monitoring agents" activities. Importantly, the failure to delegate under appropriate circumstances may constitute an abuse of discretion.

Source: The Private Trust Company

ROBERT H. BROWN, CLU, CHFC, AEP®

Bob Brown is a Registered Representative of LPL Financial Services and a licensed insurance agent and broker. He is FINRA general securities licensed and is an LPL registered financial planner. Bob is also a principal at Lehigh Valley Investment Group in Bethlehem, Pennsylvania.

His professional credentials include the Certified Life Underwriter (CLU) and the Chartered Financial Consultant (ChFC) designations from the American College in Bryn Mawr, Pennsylvania. He is also an Accredited Estate Planner (AEP) through the National Association of Estate Planners and Councils headquartered in Cleveland, Ohio. He actively pursues continuing education within the industry through these and other professional organizations.

Bob has practiced for 21 years in business as a financial advisor to individuals. He specializes in the areas of: 1) retirement planning 2) estate planning and 3) retirement income for life.

Bob is a frequent speaker at corporate and public seminars, discussing retirement planning, estate planning, long term care issues, and investments. He also conducts professional continuing education programs for CPA's and attorneys.

Made in the USA
Monee, IL
10 December 2022

20714637R00120